I0606228

From ERAS to EVER AFTER

The authorised representative in the EEA is Simon and Schuster Netherlands BV, Herculesplein 96 3584 AA Utrecht, Netherlands. (info@simonandschuster.nl)

Andrews McMeel Publishing
a division of Andrews McMeel Universal
1130 Walnut Street, Kansas City, Missouri 64106

www.andrewsmcmeel.com

Design by Melissa Gerber
Illustrations by Cinthya Álvarez

Some quotes edited for length and clarity.

26 27 28 29 30 VEP 10 9 8 7 6 5 4 3 2 1

ISBN: 979-8-8816-1157-6

Library of Congress Control Number on file.

From ERAS to EVER AFTER

LOVE NOTES FROM
TAYLOR & TRAVIS

BELLA MONTGOMERY

TABLE OF CONTENTS

A REAL LOVE STORY

Love stories captivate us because they remind us of the beauty of human existence: Two lives can collide in a way that feels inevitable, as though the universe itself conspired to bring them together. But in Taylor Swift and Travis Kelce, the world has found something rarer still. Their love story is not a fairy tale. It's real–surprising, tender, tireless, honest, and undeniable.

More than a whirlwind of public appearances, stadium moments, and irresistible headlines, theirs is a story of two people who stand in awe of one another. Taylor and Travis step into each other's worlds with curiosity and courage, never ceasing to marvel at the connection they've found. Through their words and actions, they remind us that true love is both extraordinary and simple: It is shared laughter, steadfast support, and the irrepressible joy of knowing you've met your perfect match. *From Eras to Ever After* celebrates their journey while reminding us that true love isn't reserved for fairy tales–it could be just one moment, one choice, or one heartbeat away.

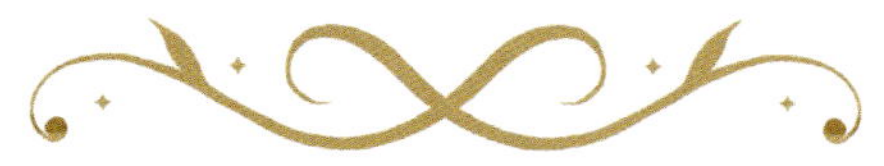

TRUE LOVE
TREASURES
THE FRIENDSHIP
BRACELET BEFORE
THE RING.

It began with a gesture so small it almost slipped away: a friendship bracelet, strung with intention, waiting to carry a phone number across a stadium crowd. A shot in the dark. Travis confessed that he had tried (and failed) to deliver a friendship bracelet with his phone number to Taylor at her Eras Tour show in Kansas City. But love has a way of finding its moment. When Taylor later called his bold move "metal as hell," a playful spark turned into something much greater than either could have imagined. It all happened very organically, Travis says. "We fell in love just based off the people we were sitting in a room together with. . . . We share all those values."

TRUE LOVE DOESN'T NEED AN AUDIENCE.

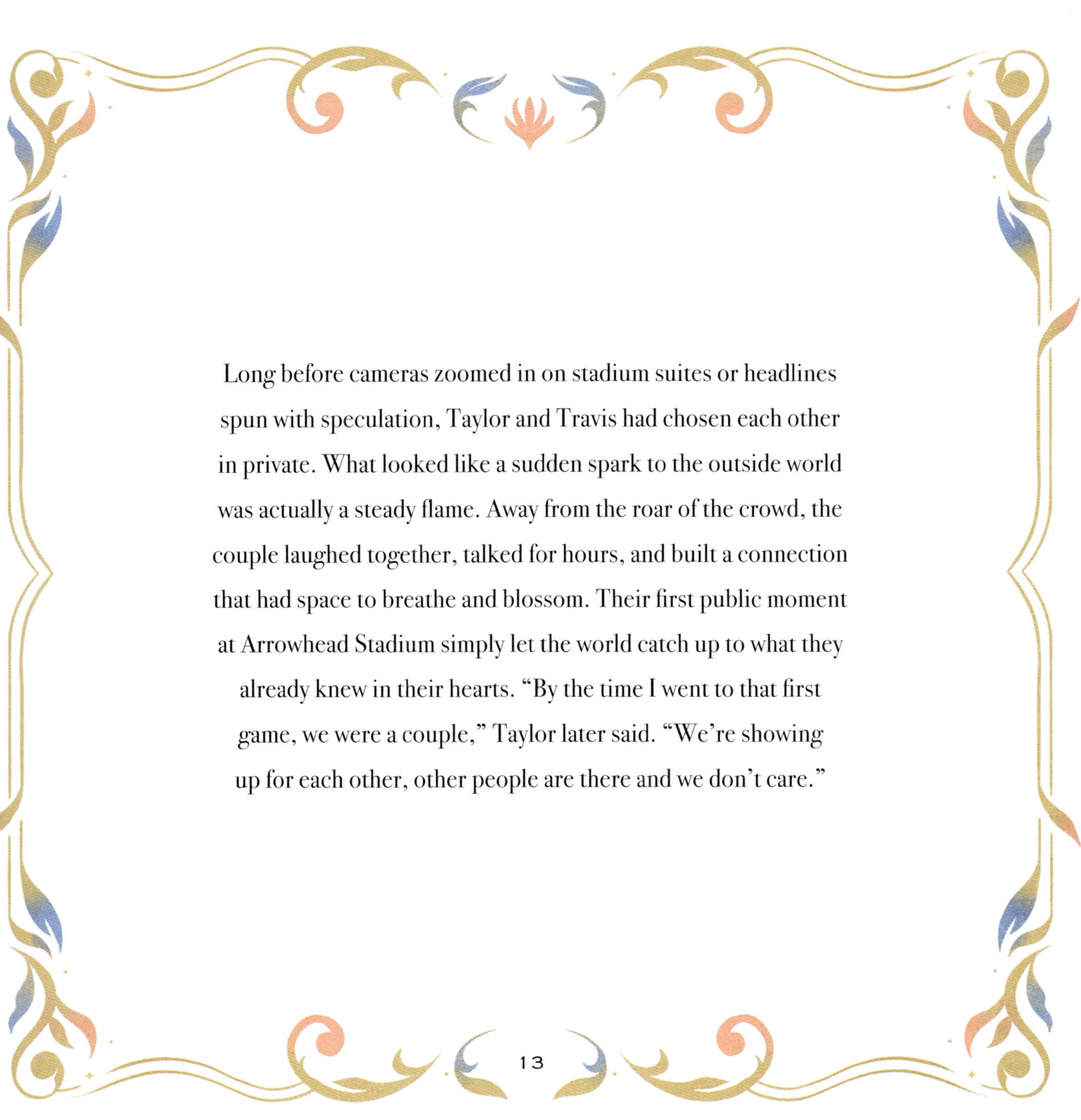

Long before cameras zoomed in on stadium suites or headlines spun with speculation, Taylor and Travis had chosen each other in private. What looked like a sudden spark to the outside world was actually a steady flame. Away from the roar of the crowd, the couple laughed together, talked for hours, and built a connection that had space to breathe and blossom. Their first public moment at Arrowhead Stadium simply let the world catch up to what they already knew in their hearts. "By the time I went to that first game, we were a couple," Taylor later said. "We're showing up for each other, other people are there and we don't care."

"She blew me away, and I'd never experienced something so mesmerizing on stage and then so real and so beautiful in person."

—TRAVIS

"It was such a wild romantic gesture, to just be like, 'I want to date you!'"

—TAYLOR

TRUE LOVE MAKES THE FIRST CONVERSATION FEEL LIKE THE MILLIONTH.

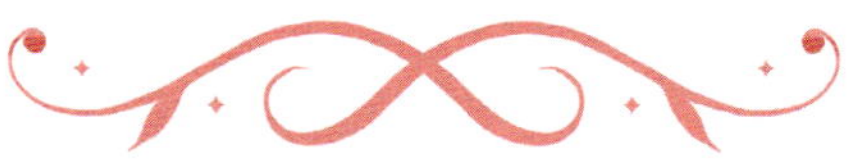

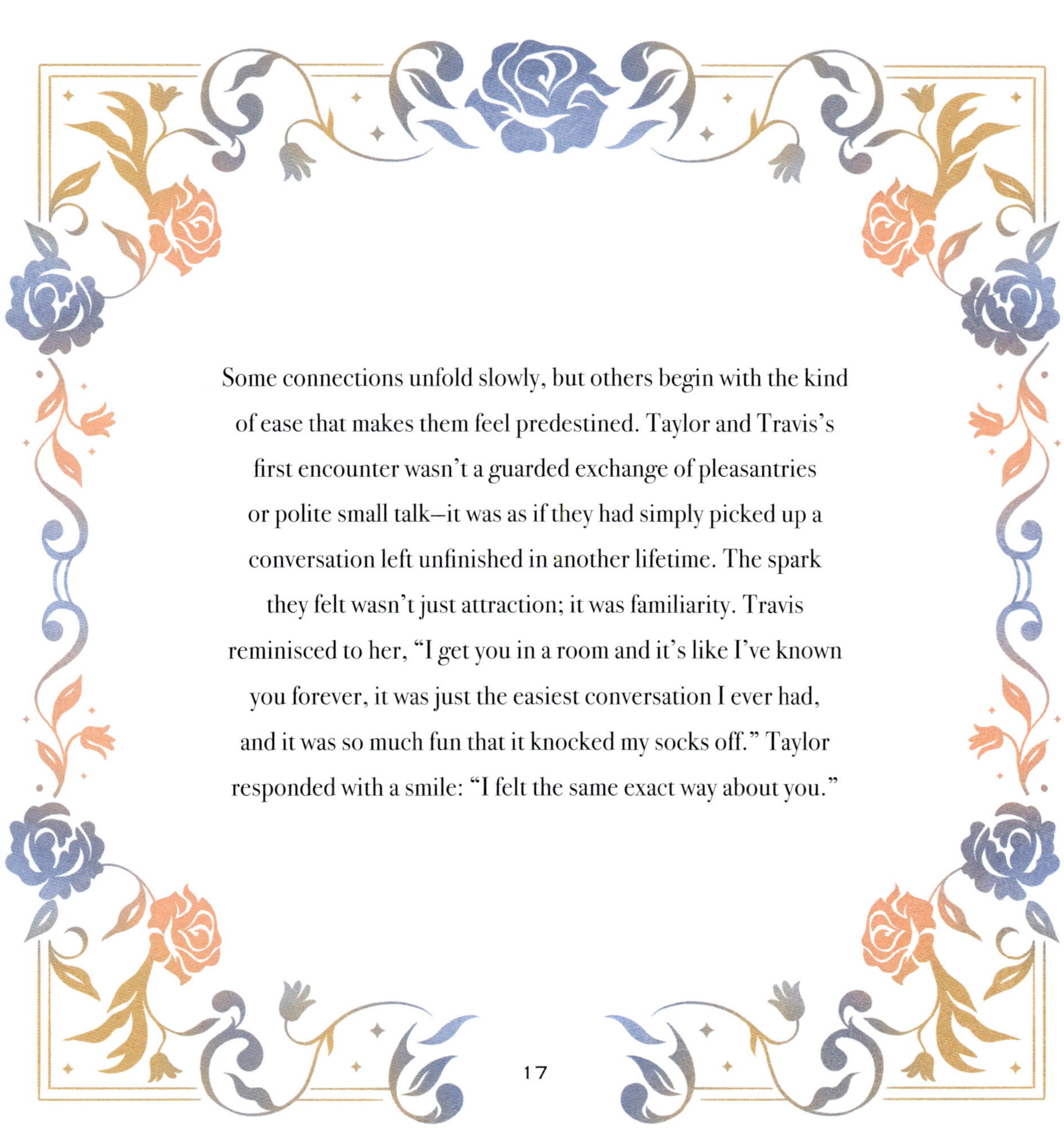

Some connections unfold slowly, but others begin with the kind of ease that makes them feel predestined. Taylor and Travis's first encounter wasn't a guarded exchange of pleasantries or polite small talk–it was as if they had simply picked up a conversation left unfinished in another lifetime. The spark they felt wasn't just attraction; it was familiarity. Travis reminisced to her, "I get you in a room and it's like I've known you forever, it was just the easiest conversation I ever had, and it was so much fun that it knocked my socks off." Taylor responded with a smile: "I felt the same exact way about you."

TRUE LOVE STANDS IN AWE.

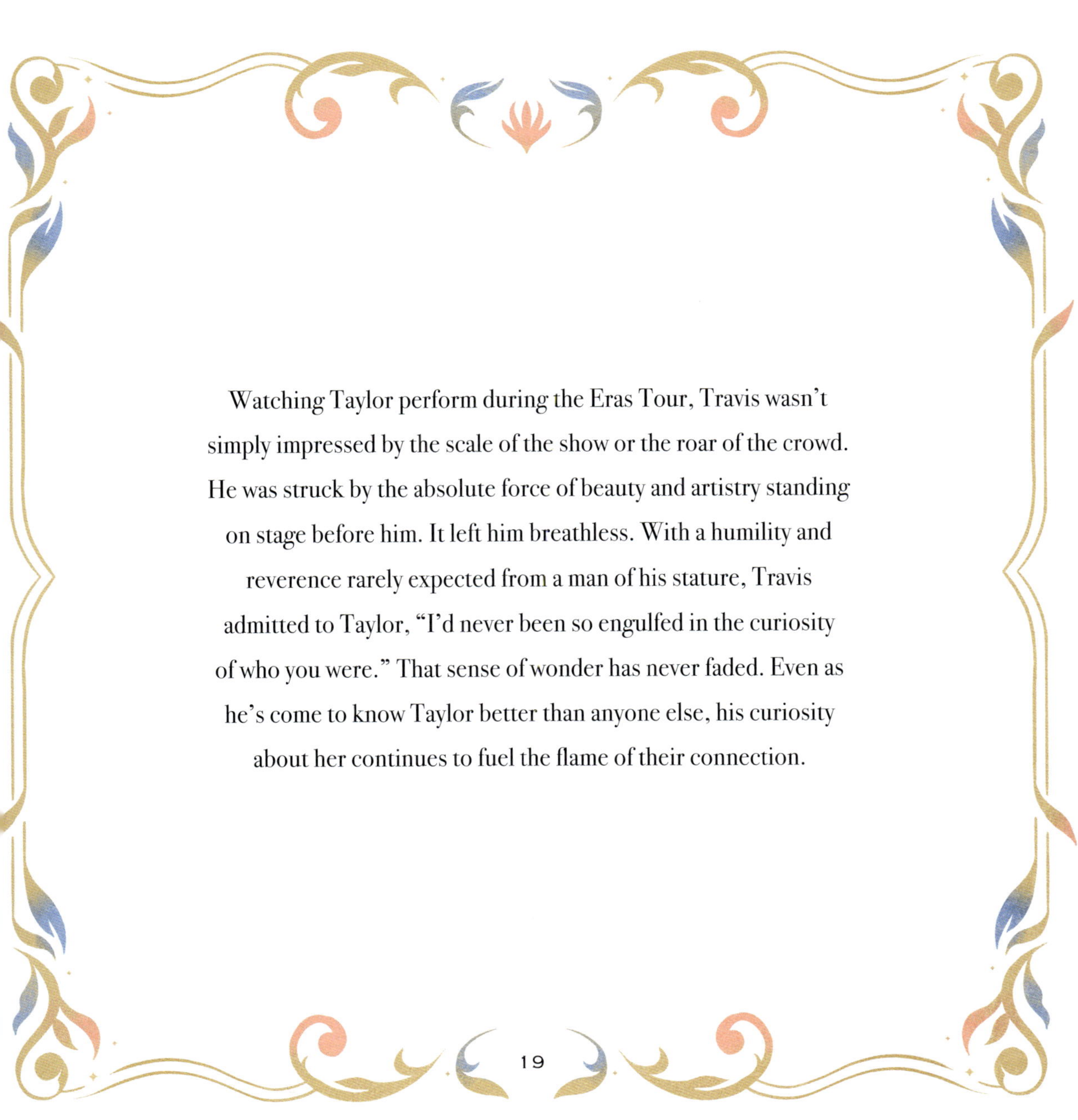

Watching Taylor perform during the Eras Tour, Travis wasn't simply impressed by the scale of the show or the roar of the crowd. He was struck by the absolute force of beauty and artistry standing on stage before him. It left him breathless. With a humility and reverence rarely expected from a man of his stature, Travis admitted to Taylor, "I'd never been so engulfed in the curiosity of who you were." That sense of wonder has never faded. Even as he's come to know Taylor better than anyone else, his curiosity about her continues to fuel the flame of their connection.

TRUE LOVE IS A SAFE HARBOR.

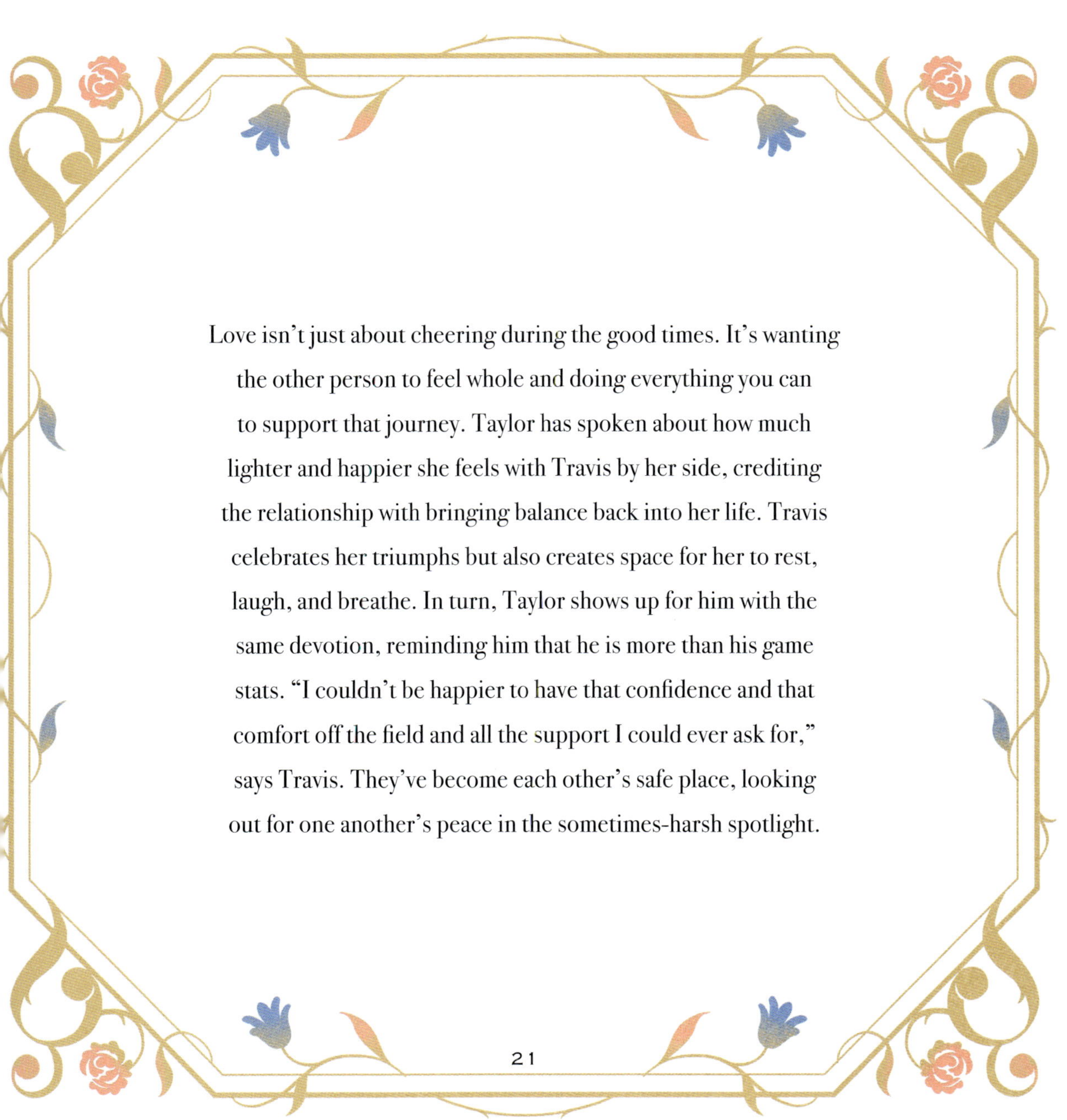

Love isn't just about cheering during the good times. It's wanting the other person to feel whole and doing everything you can to support that journey. Taylor has spoken about how much lighter and happier she feels with Travis by her side, crediting the relationship with bringing balance back into her life. Travis celebrates her triumphs but also creates space for her to rest, laugh, and breathe. In turn, Taylor shows up for him with the same devotion, reminding him that he is more than his game stats. "I couldn't be happier to have that confidence and that comfort off the field and all the support I could ever ask for," says Travis. They've become each other's safe place, looking out for one another's peace in the sometimes-harsh spotlight.

“He thought because he knows the elevator lady that he could talk to her about just getting down to my dressing room. That’s how it [worked] in 1973. He was really just like, ‘I know a guy, I can figure this out.’”

—Taylor

"I did the whole friendship bracelet thing and told everyone how butthurt I was that I didn't get to meet Taylor."

—Travis

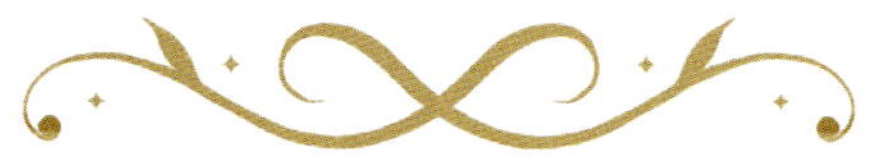

TRUE LOVE
DRAWS YOU
CLOSER.

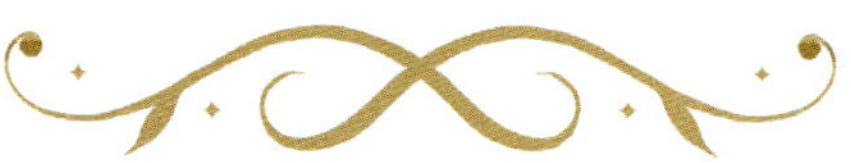

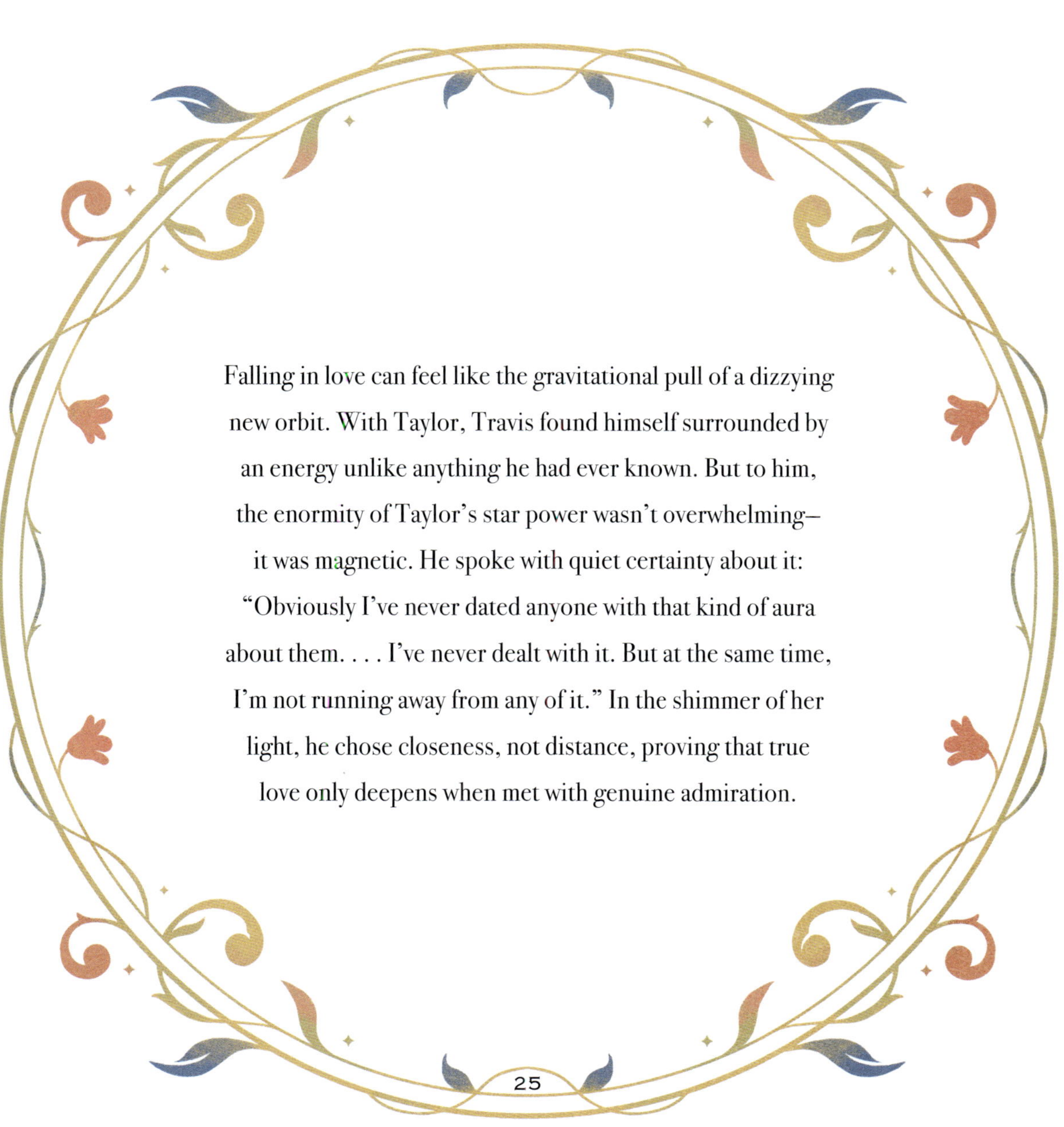

Falling in love can feel like the gravitational pull of a dizzying new orbit. With Taylor, Travis found himself surrounded by an energy unlike anything he had ever known. But to him, the enormity of Taylor's star power wasn't overwhelming–it was magnetic. He spoke with quiet certainty about it: "Obviously I've never dated anyone with that kind of aura about them. . . . I've never dealt with it. But at the same time, I'm not running away from any of it." In the shimmer of her light, he chose closeness, not distance, proving that true love only deepens when met with genuine admiration.

TRUE LOVE SEEKS YOUR LIGHT OVER CAMERA FLASHES.

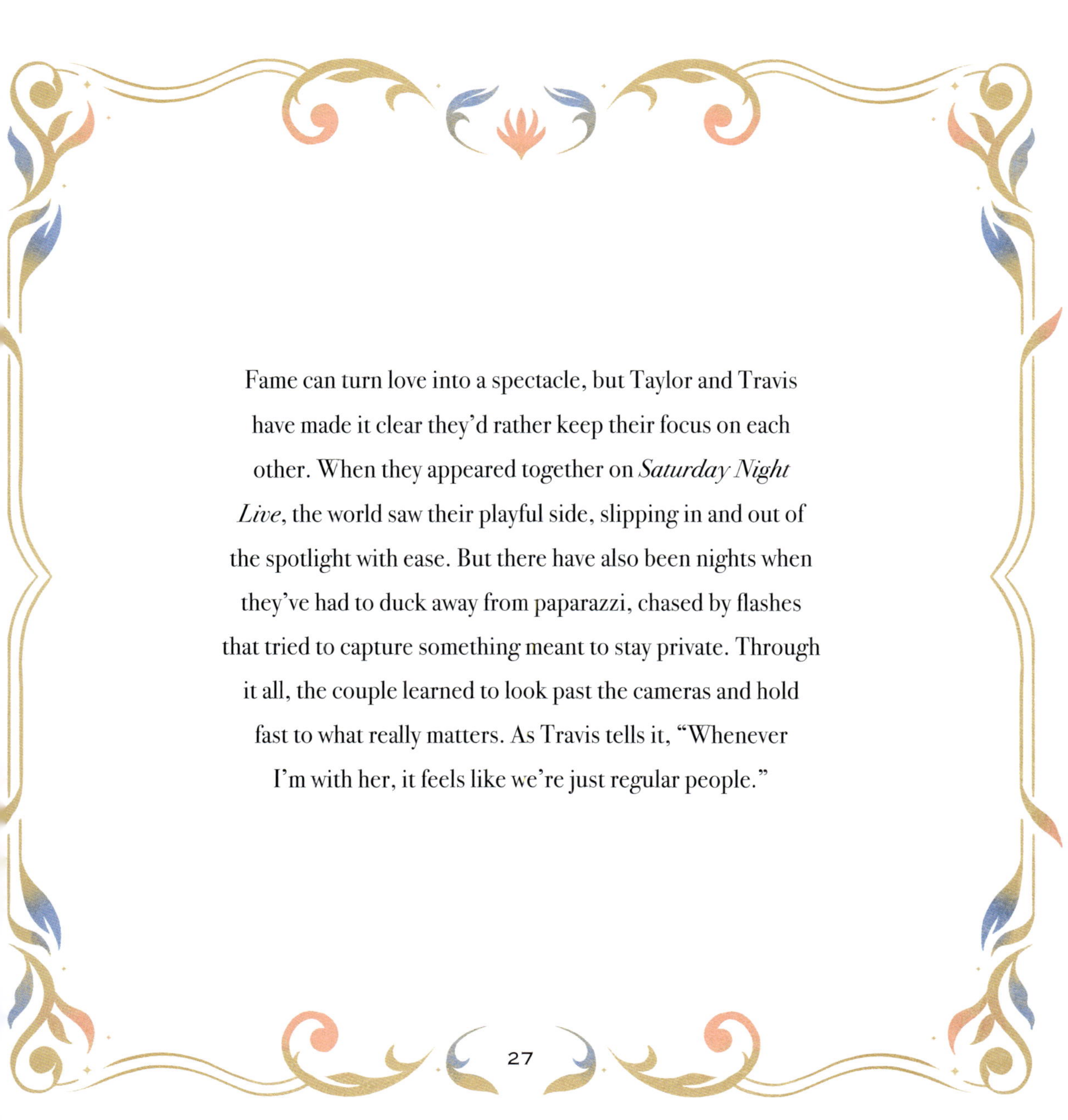

Fame can turn love into a spectacle, but Taylor and Travis have made it clear they'd rather keep their focus on each other. When they appeared together on *Saturday Night Live*, the world saw their playful side, slipping in and out of the spotlight with ease. But there have also been nights when they've had to duck away from paparazzi, chased by flashes that tried to capture something meant to stay private. Through it all, the couple learned to look past the cameras and hold fast to what really matters. As Travis tells it, "Whenever I'm with her, it feels like we're just regular people."

"When there is not a camera on us, we're just two people that are in love."

—Travis

"We actually had a significant amount of time that no one knew, which I'm grateful for, because we got to get to know each other."

—TAYLOR

TRUE LOVE BRINGS OUT THE BEST IN YOU.

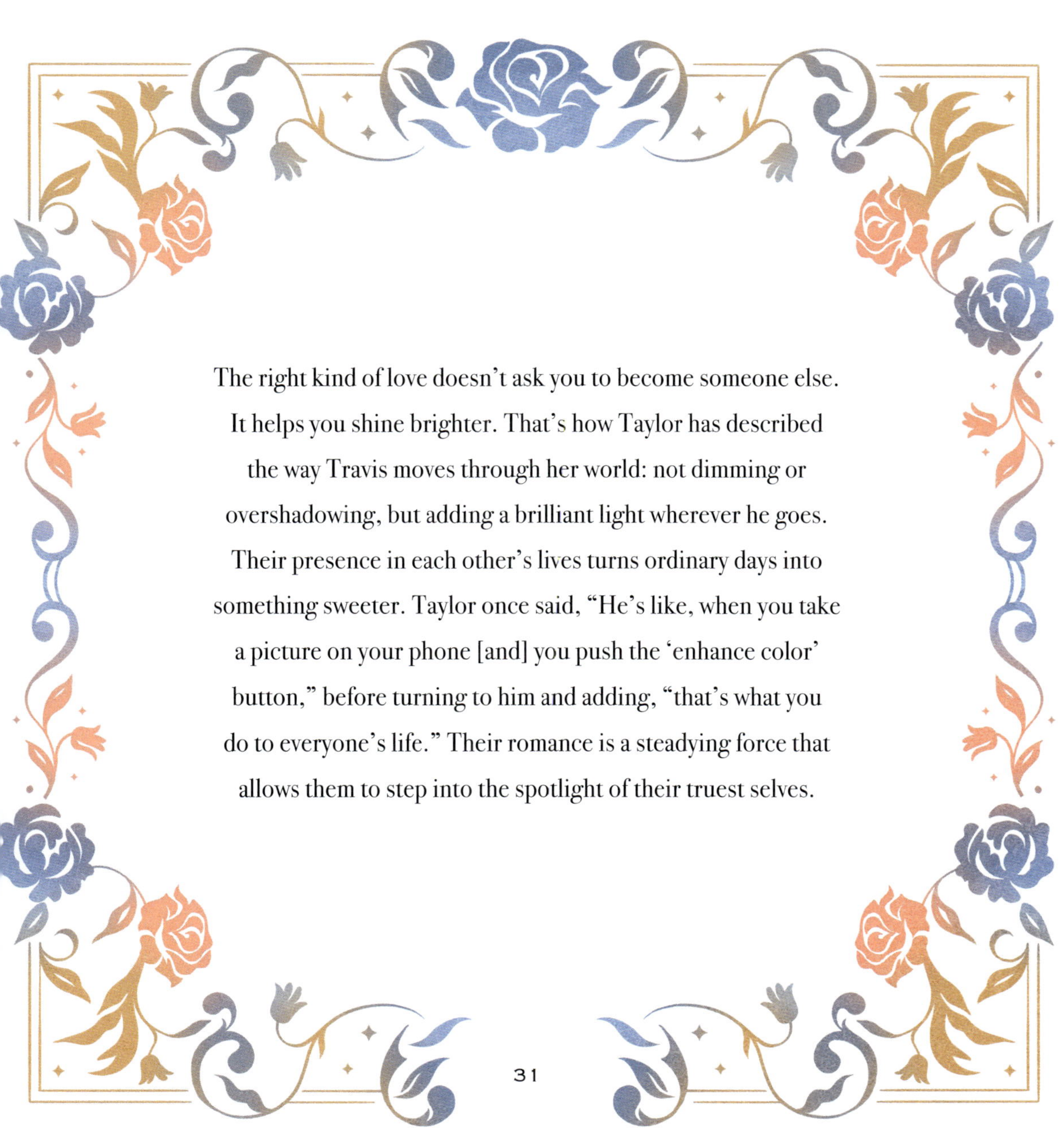

The right kind of love doesn't ask you to become someone else. It helps you shine brighter. That's how Taylor has described the way Travis moves through her world: not dimming or overshadowing, but adding a brilliant light wherever he goes. Their presence in each other's lives turns ordinary days into something sweeter. Taylor once said, "He's like, when you take a picture on your phone [and] you push the 'enhance color' button," before turning to him and adding, "that's what you do to everyone's life." Their romance is a steadying force that allows them to step into the spotlight of their truest selves.

TRUE LOVE SPARKS NEW DISCOVERIES.

Love invites you into places and passions you may never have expected. For Taylor, that has meant trading stadium stages for stadium suites, learning the rhythms of the game Travis has devoted his life to, and cheering him on. What started as simple encouragement grew into genuine excitement, as she admitted, "Football is awesome, it turns out." For Travis, the discoveries were just as sweet—standing in packed arenas, he watched her turn lyrics into anthems for tens of thousands. He's also stepped onto her stage in London, glimpsed the devotion of her fans, and seen firsthand the magic she creates night after night. Together, they've found joy in what the other loves most and a shared story of music, football, and forever.

TRUE LOVE
MAKES YOU
FEEL LIKE PART
OF A TEAM.

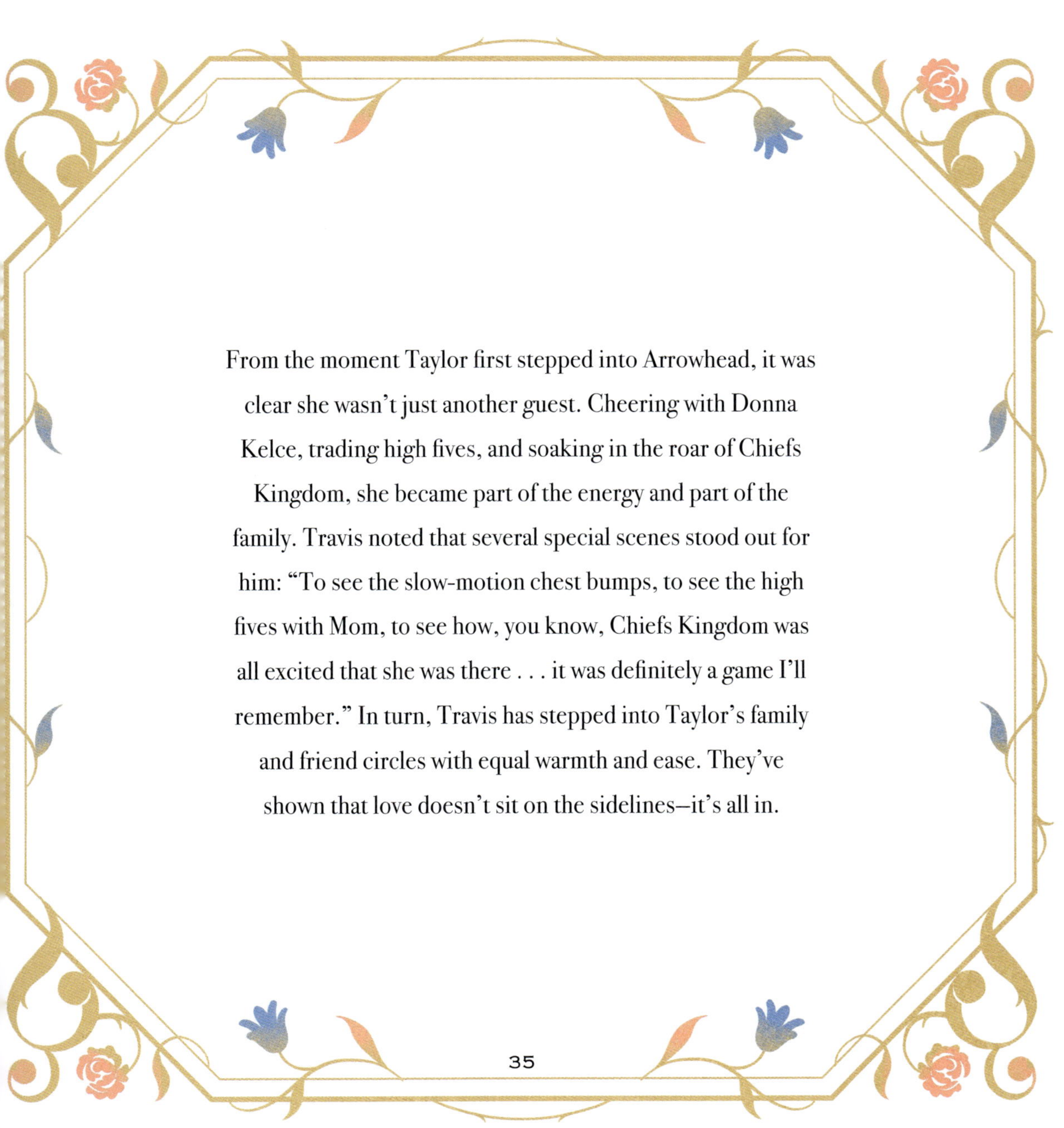

From the moment Taylor first stepped into Arrowhead, it was clear she wasn't just another guest. Cheering with Donna Kelce, trading high fives, and soaking in the roar of Chiefs Kingdom, she became part of the energy and part of the family. Travis noted that several special scenes stood out for him: "To see the slow-motion chest bumps, to see the high fives with Mom, to see how, you know, Chiefs Kingdom was all excited that she was there . . . it was definitely a game I'll remember." In turn, Travis has stepped into Taylor's family and friend circles with equal warmth and ease. They've shown that love doesn't sit on the sidelines–it's all in.

"He's a human exclamation point."

—TAYLOR

"She is the most engulfed fan now . . . she just naturally loves to hear about my job."

—TRAVIS

TRUE LOVE CELEBRATES EVERY WIN.

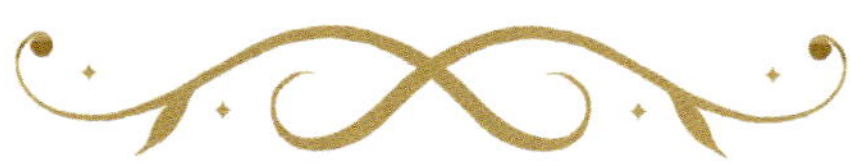

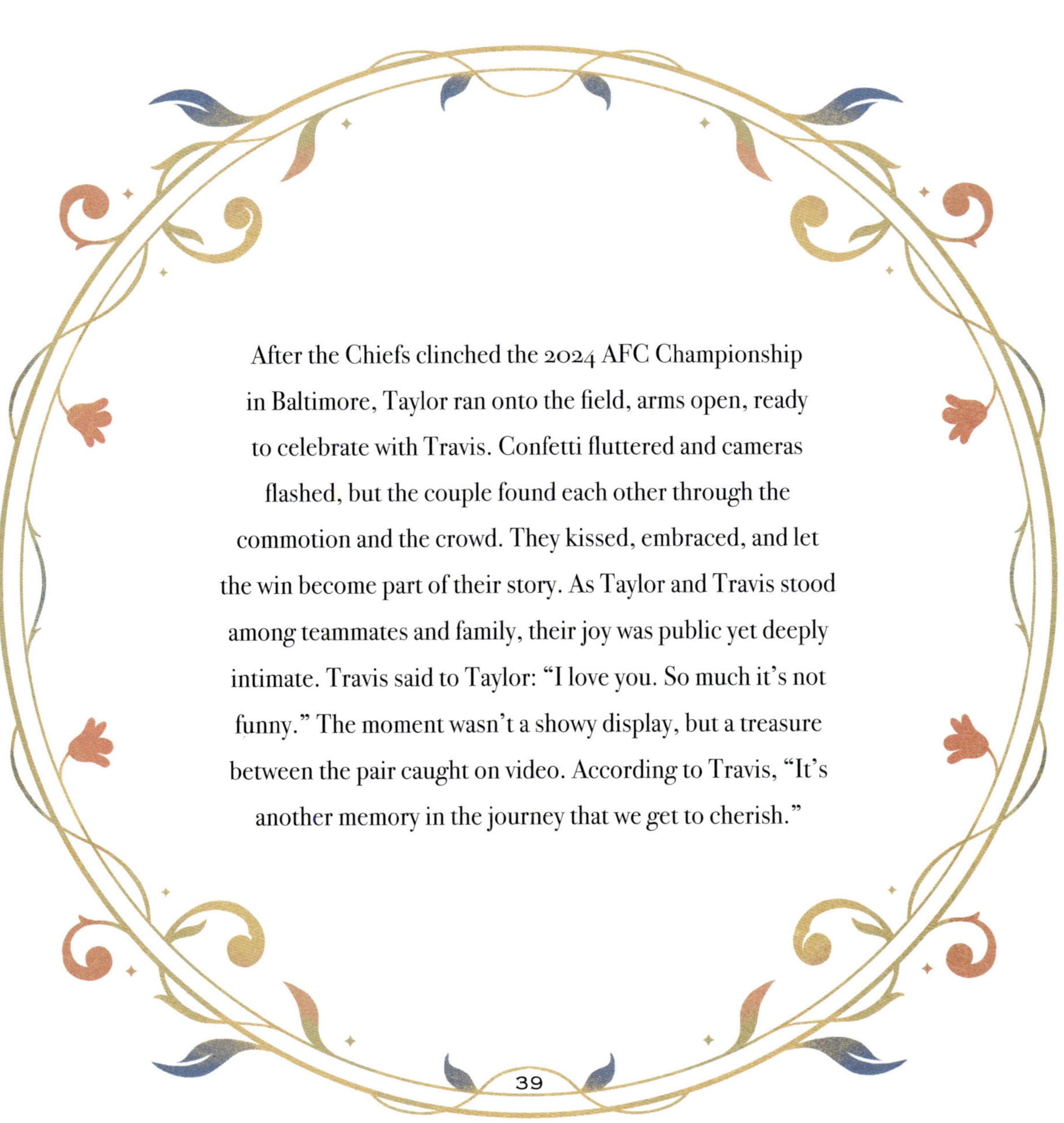

After the Chiefs clinched the 2024 AFC Championship in Baltimore, Taylor ran onto the field, arms open, ready to celebrate with Travis. Confetti fluttered and cameras flashed, but the couple found each other through the commotion and the crowd. They kissed, embraced, and let the win become part of their story. As Taylor and Travis stood among teammates and family, their joy was public yet deeply intimate. Travis said to Taylor: "I love you. So much it's not funny." The moment wasn't a showy display, but a treasure between the pair caught on video. According to Travis, "It's another memory in the journey that we get to cherish."

TRUE
LOVE
SURPRISES
YOU.

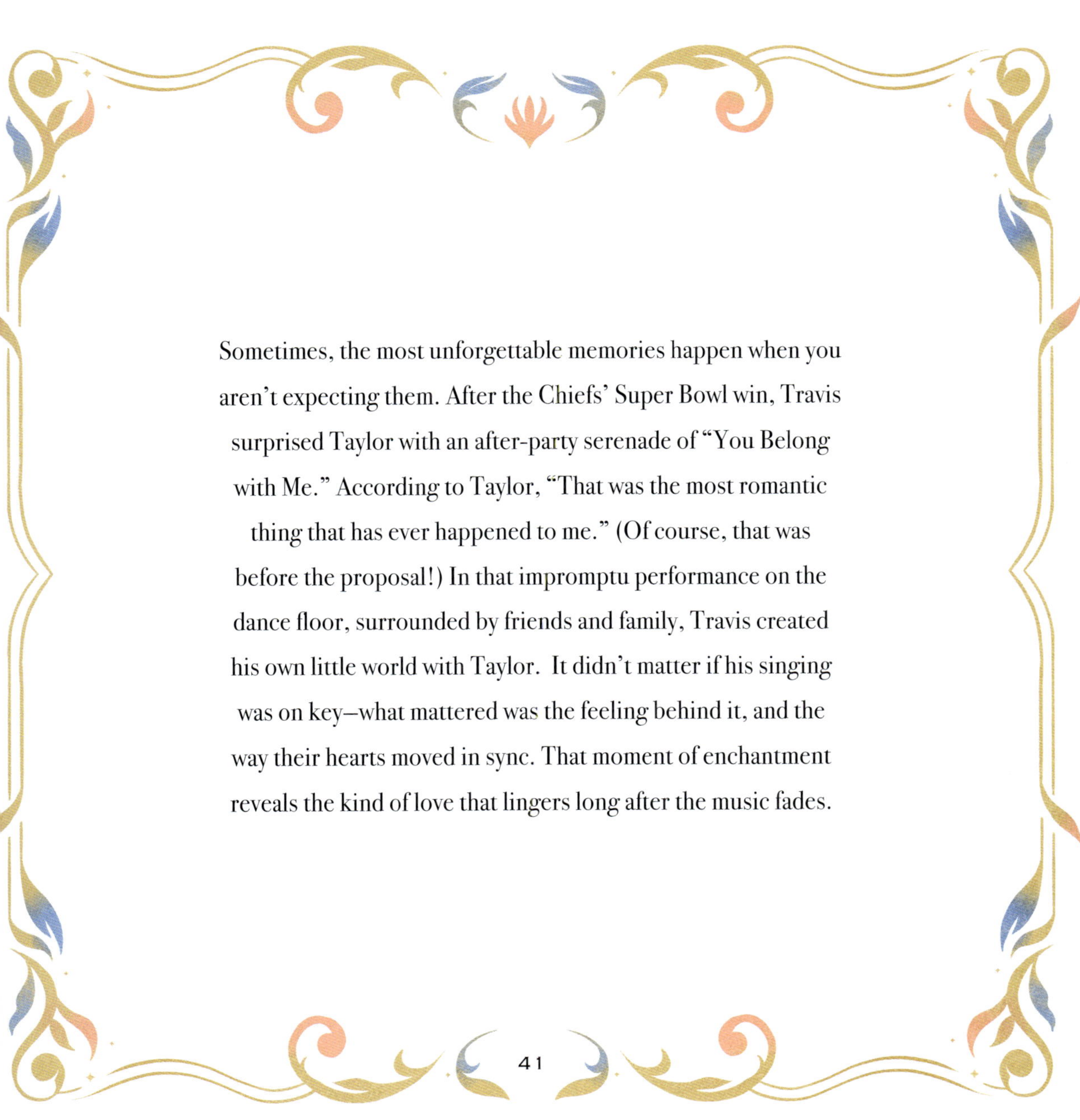

Sometimes, the most unforgettable memories happen when you aren't expecting them. After the Chiefs' Super Bowl win, Travis surprised Taylor with an after-party serenade of "You Belong with Me." According to Taylor, "That was the most romantic thing that has ever happened to me." (Of course, that was before the proposal!) In that impromptu performance on the dance floor, surrounded by friends and family, Travis created his own little world with Taylor. It didn't matter if his singing was on key–what mattered was the feeling behind it, and the way their hearts moved in sync. That moment of enchantment reveals the kind of love that lingers long after the music fades.

"We met in the middle and I was like: 'What is happening in my life right now?!'"

—Taylor

"It's been a crazy, crazy ride that I could have never anticipated."

—TRAVIS

TRUE LOVE NOTICES THE LITTLE THINGS.

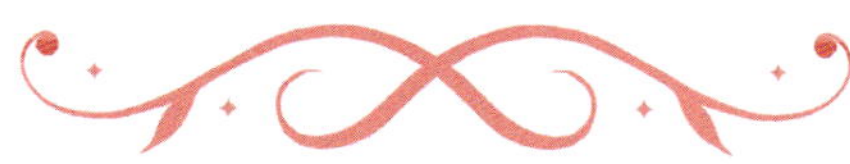

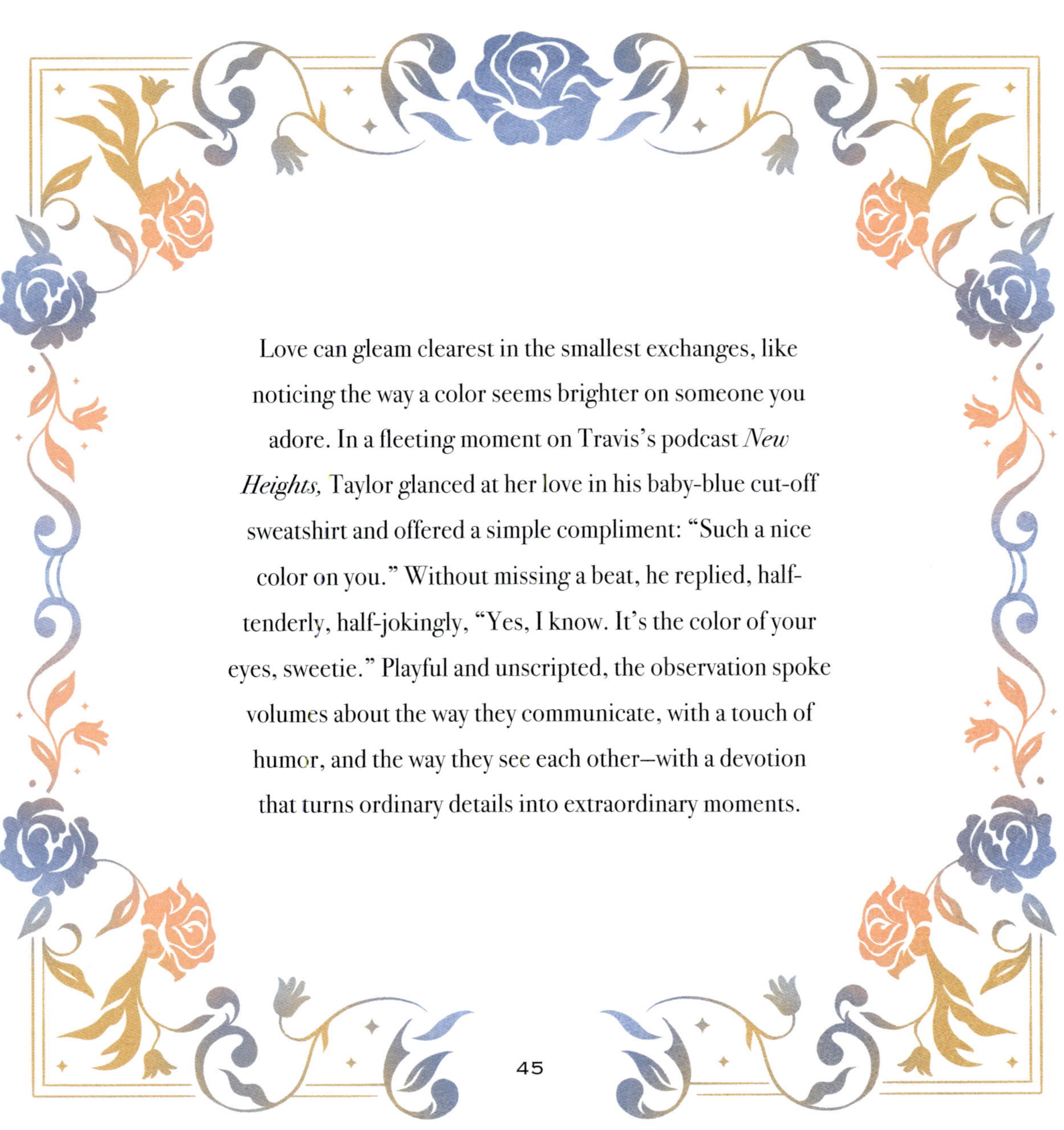

Love can gleam clearest in the smallest exchanges, like noticing the way a color seems brighter on someone you adore. In a fleeting moment on Travis's podcast *New Heights,* Taylor glanced at her love in his baby-blue cut-off sweatshirt and offered a simple compliment: "Such a nice color on you." Without missing a beat, he replied, half-tenderly, half-jokingly, "Yes, I know. It's the color of your eyes, sweetie." Playful and unscripted, the observation spoke volumes about the way they communicate, with a touch of humor, and the way they see each other–with a devotion that turns ordinary details into extraordinary moments.

TRUE LOVE
DREAMS
WITH YOU.

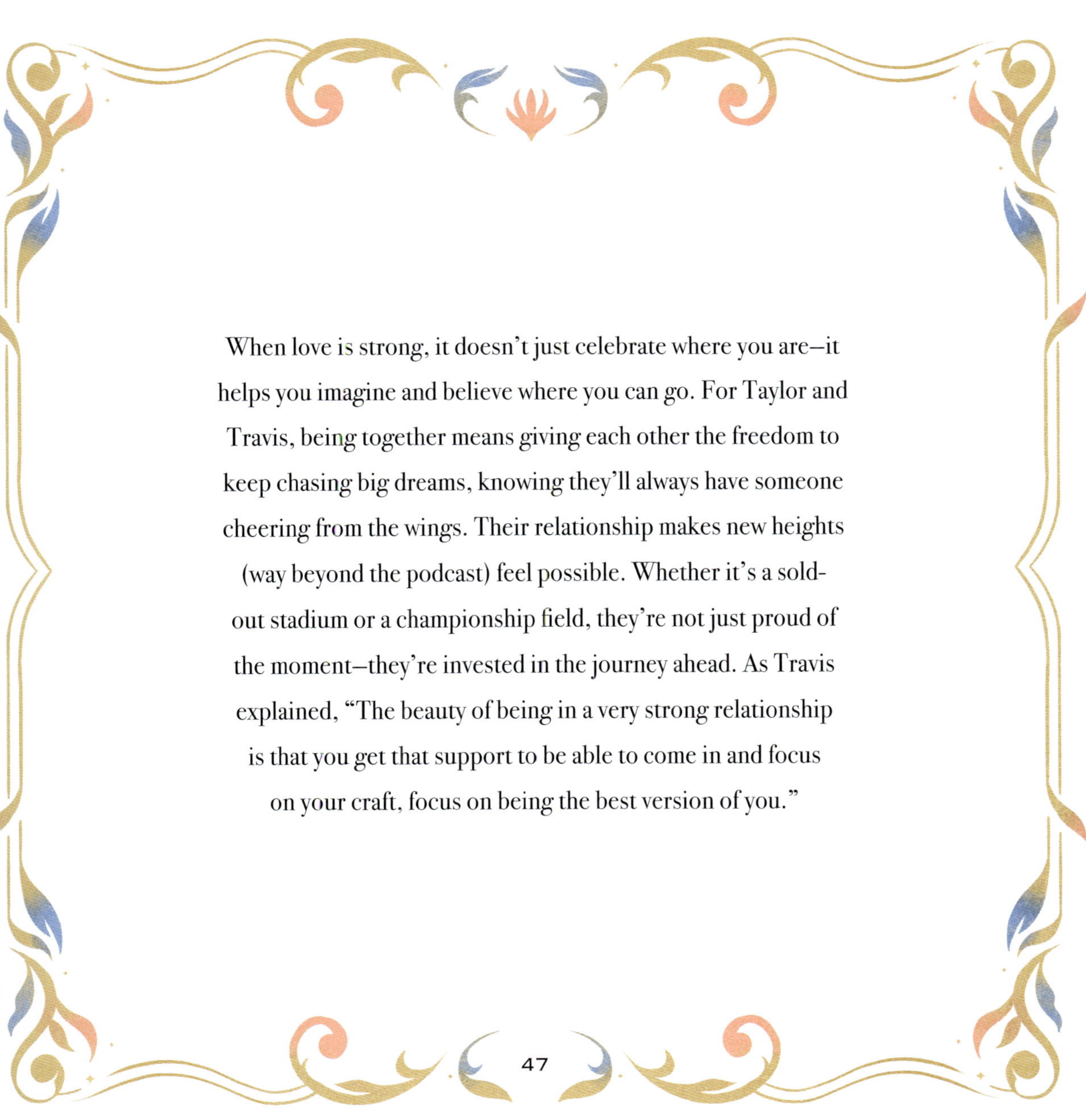

When love is strong, it doesn't just celebrate where you are—it helps you imagine and believe where you can go. For Taylor and Travis, being together means giving each other the freedom to keep chasing big dreams, knowing they'll always have someone cheering from the wings. Their relationship makes new heights (way beyond the podcast) feel possible. Whether it's a sold-out stadium or a championship field, they're not just proud of the moment—they're invested in the journey ahead. As Travis explained, "The beauty of being in a very strong relationship is that you get that support to be able to come in and focus on your craft, focus on being the best version of you."

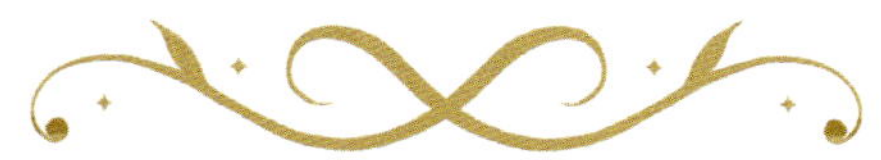

TRUE LOVE
MAKES YOU FEEL
FOREVER YOUNG.

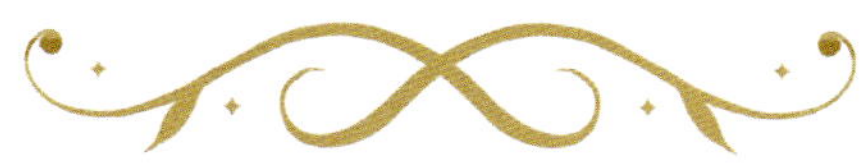

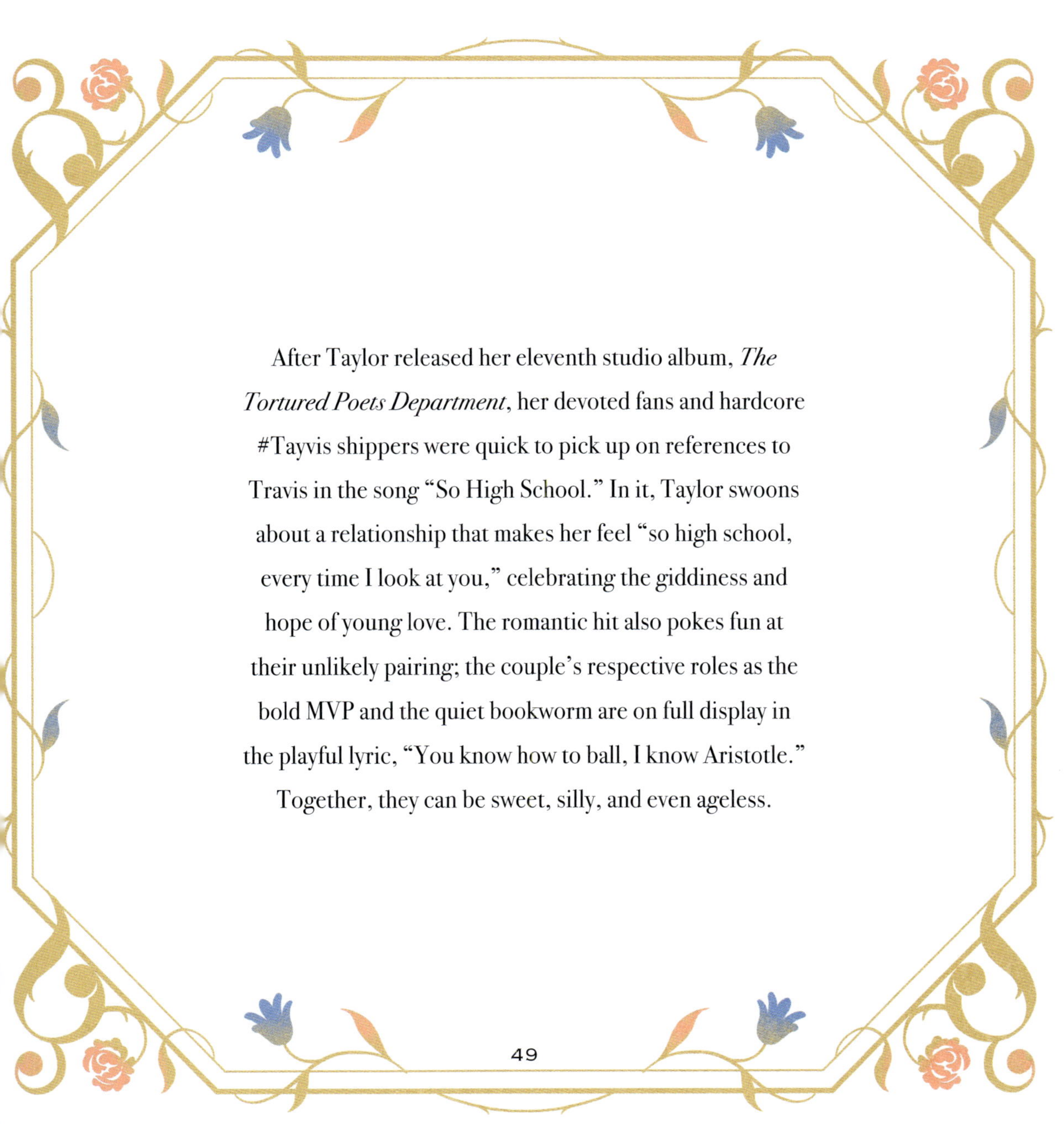

After Taylor released her eleventh studio album, *The Tortured Poets Department*, her devoted fans and hardcore #Tayvis shippers were quick to pick up on references to Travis in the song "So High School." In it, Taylor swoons about a relationship that makes her feel "so high school, every time I look at you," celebrating the giddiness and hope of young love. The romantic hit also pokes fun at their unlikely pairing; the couple's respective roles as the bold MVP and the quiet bookworm are on full display in the playful lyric, "You know how to ball, I know Aristotle." Together, they can be sweet, silly, and even ageless.

"There are no rules when it comes to love. I just try to let love surprise me because you never know who you're going to fall in love with. You never know who's going to come into your life."

—Taylor

"She's very self-aware. And I think that's why I really started to really fall for her—[it] was how genuine she is around friends [and] family."

—Travis

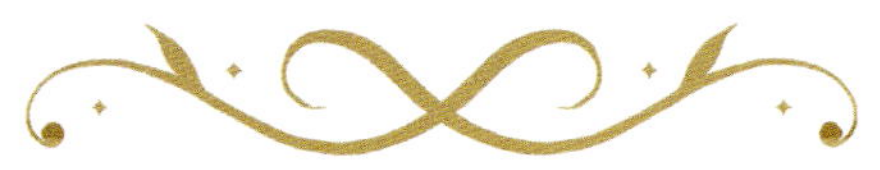

TRUE LOVE CROSSES OCEANS AND TIME ZONES.

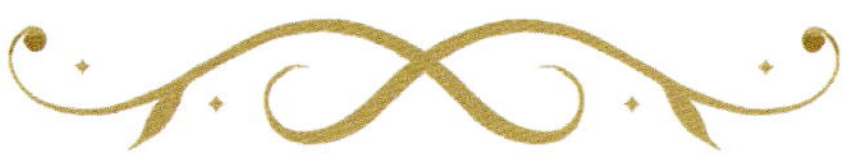

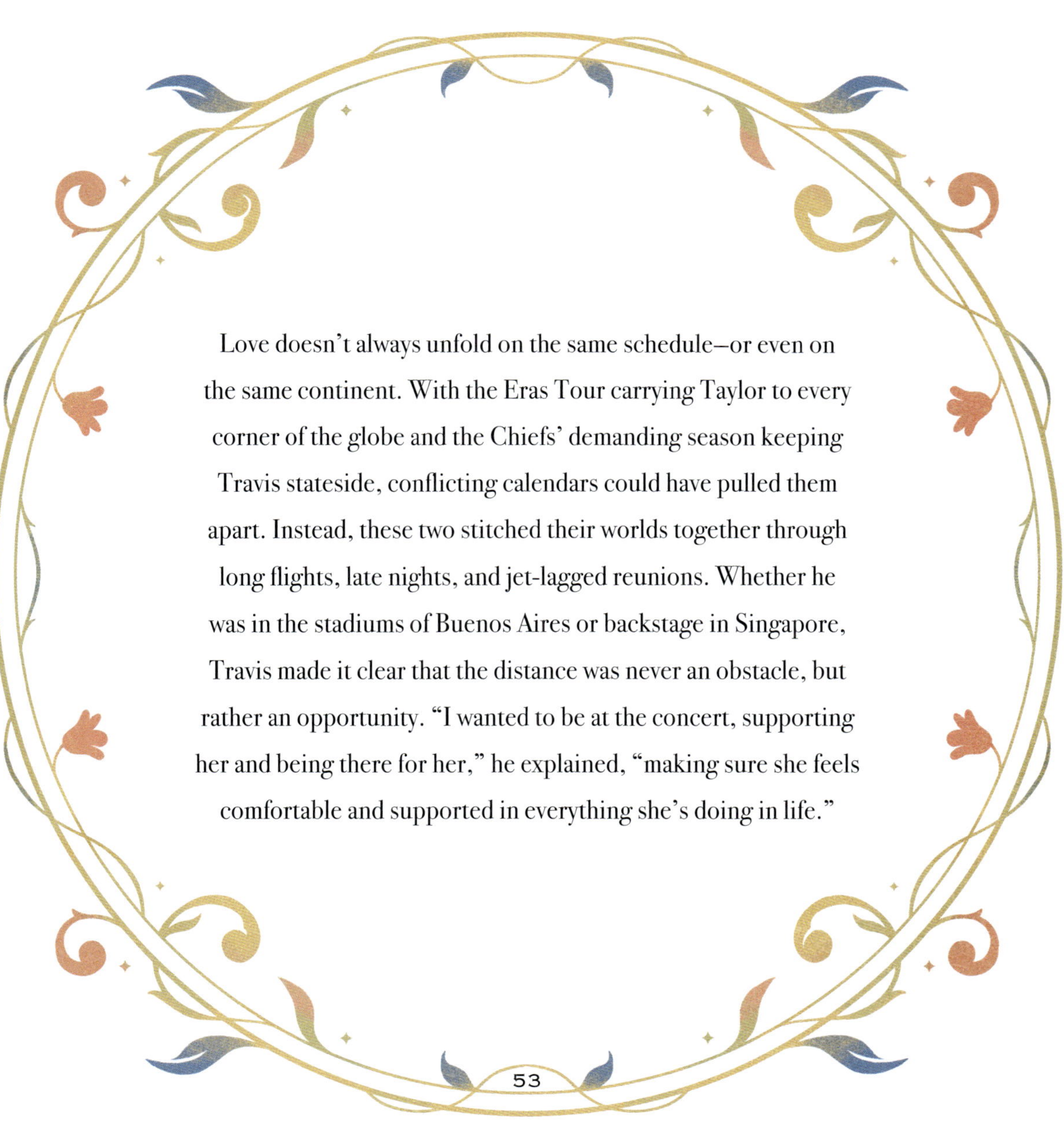

Love doesn't always unfold on the same schedule—or even on the same continent. With the Eras Tour carrying Taylor to every corner of the globe and the Chiefs' demanding season keeping Travis stateside, conflicting calendars could have pulled them apart. Instead, these two stitched their worlds together through long flights, late nights, and jet-lagged reunions. Whether he was in the stadiums of Buenos Aires or backstage in Singapore, Travis made it clear that the distance was never an obstacle, but rather an opportunity. "I wanted to be at the concert, supporting her and being there for her," he explained, "making sure she feels comfortable and supported in everything she's doing in life."

TRUE LOVE
STEPS INTO
YOUR WORLD.

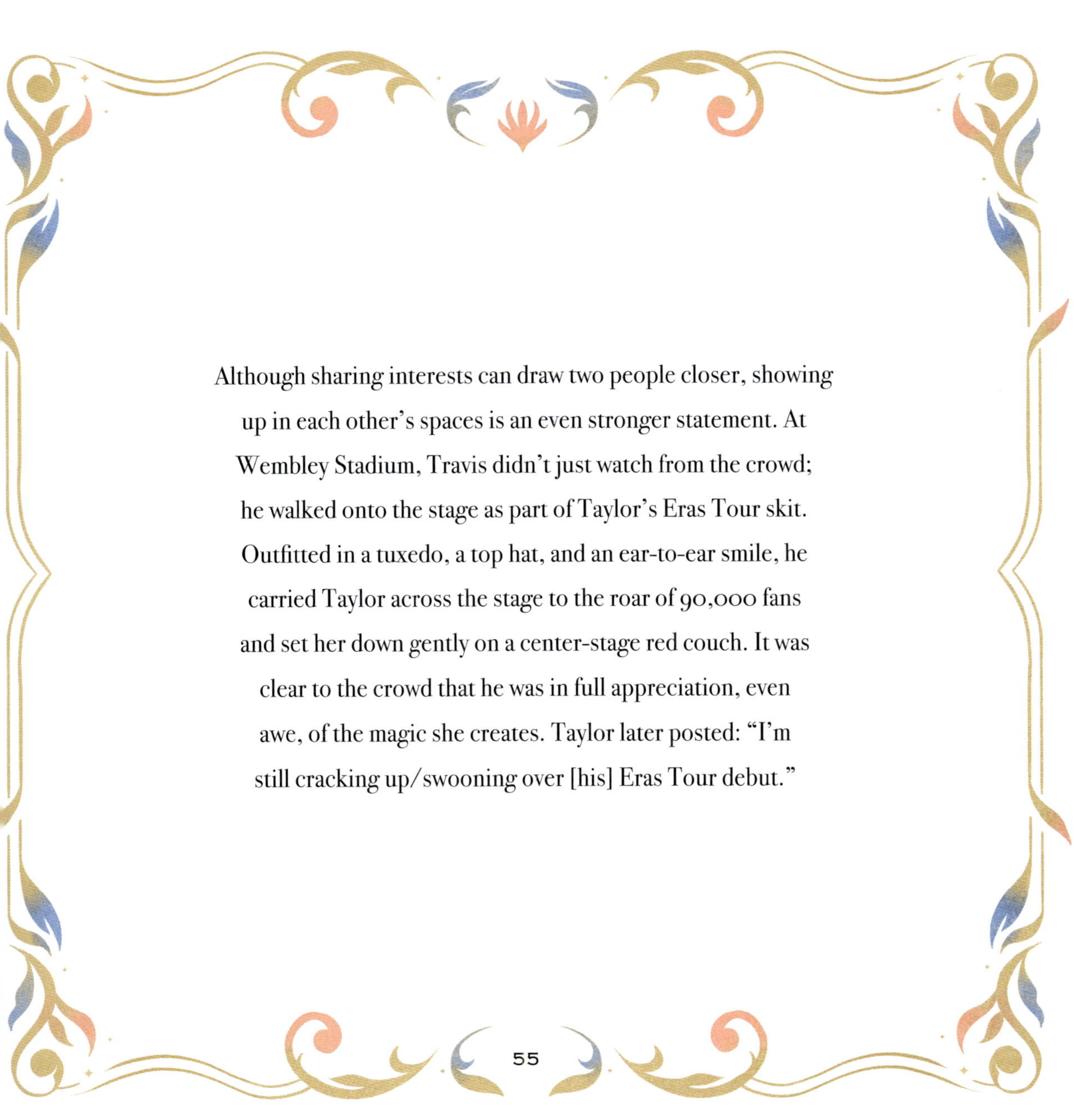

Although sharing interests can draw two people closer, showing up in each other's spaces is an even stronger statement. At Wembley Stadium, Travis didn't just watch from the crowd; he walked onto the stage as part of Taylor's Eras Tour skit. Outfitted in a tuxedo, a top hat, and an ear-to-ear smile, he carried Taylor across the stage to the roar of 90,000 fans and set her down gently on a center-stage red couch. It was clear to the crowd that he was in full appreciation, even awe, of the magic she creates. Taylor later posted: "I'm still cracking up/swooning over [his] Eras Tour debut."

"I'm just enjoying the fun of being at this really cool event that I always wanted to go to with the person that I love."

—Travis

"Life is short. Have adventures. Me locking myself away in my house for a lot of years—I'll never get that time back. I'm more trusting now than I was six years ago."

—Taylor

TRUE LOVE
ALWAYS ROOTS
FOR YOU
AS YOUR
BIGGEST FAN.

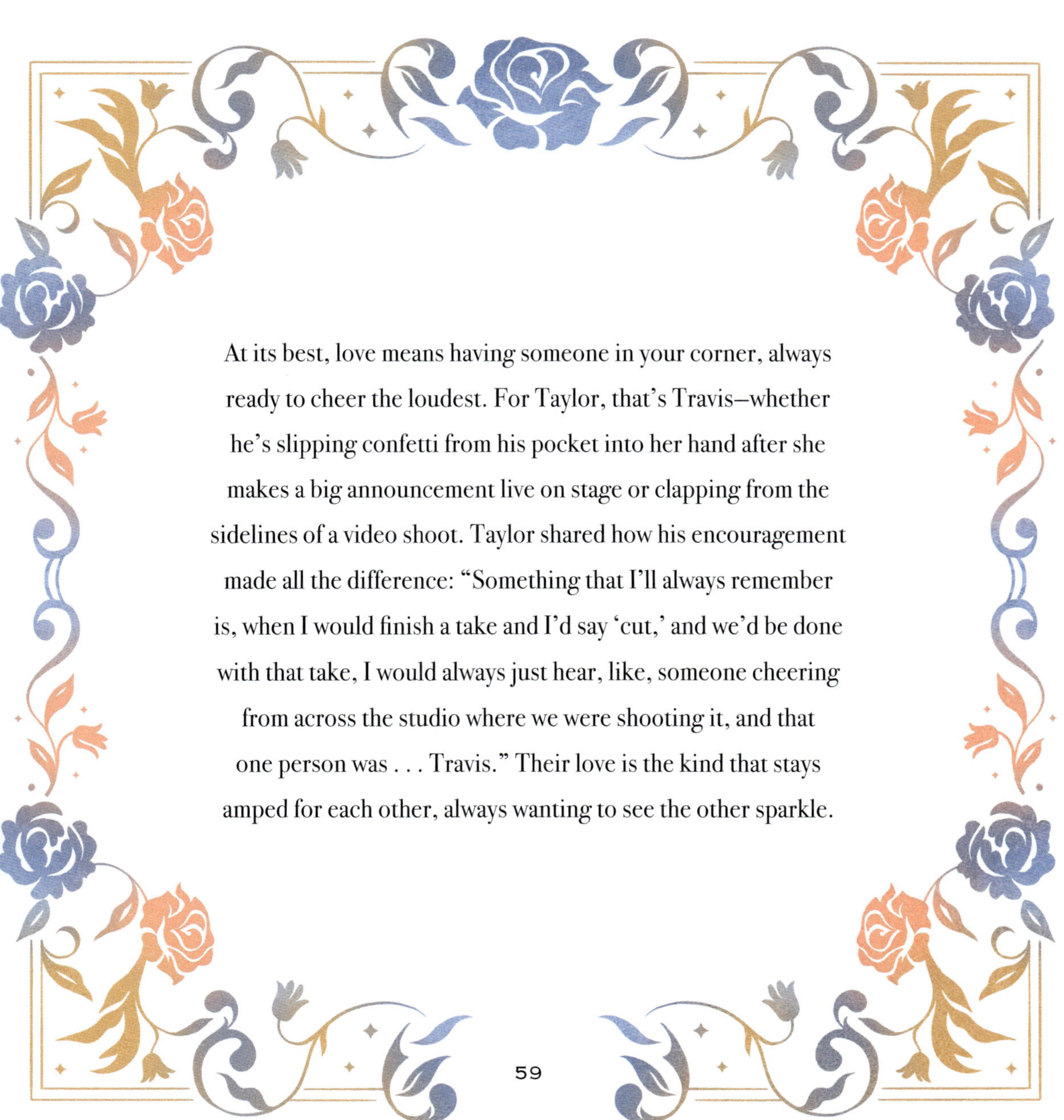

At its best, love means having someone in your corner, always ready to cheer the loudest. For Taylor, that's Travis—whether he's slipping confetti from his pocket into her hand after she makes a big announcement live on stage or clapping from the sidelines of a video shoot. Taylor shared how his encouragement made all the difference: "Something that I'll always remember is, when I would finish a take and I'd say 'cut,' and we'd be done with that take, I would always just hear, like, someone cheering from across the studio where we were shooting it, and that one person was . . . Travis." Their love is the kind that stays amped for each other, always wanting to see the other sparkle.

TRUE LOVE HELPS YOU SEE YOURSELF IN A BRAND-NEW LIGHT.

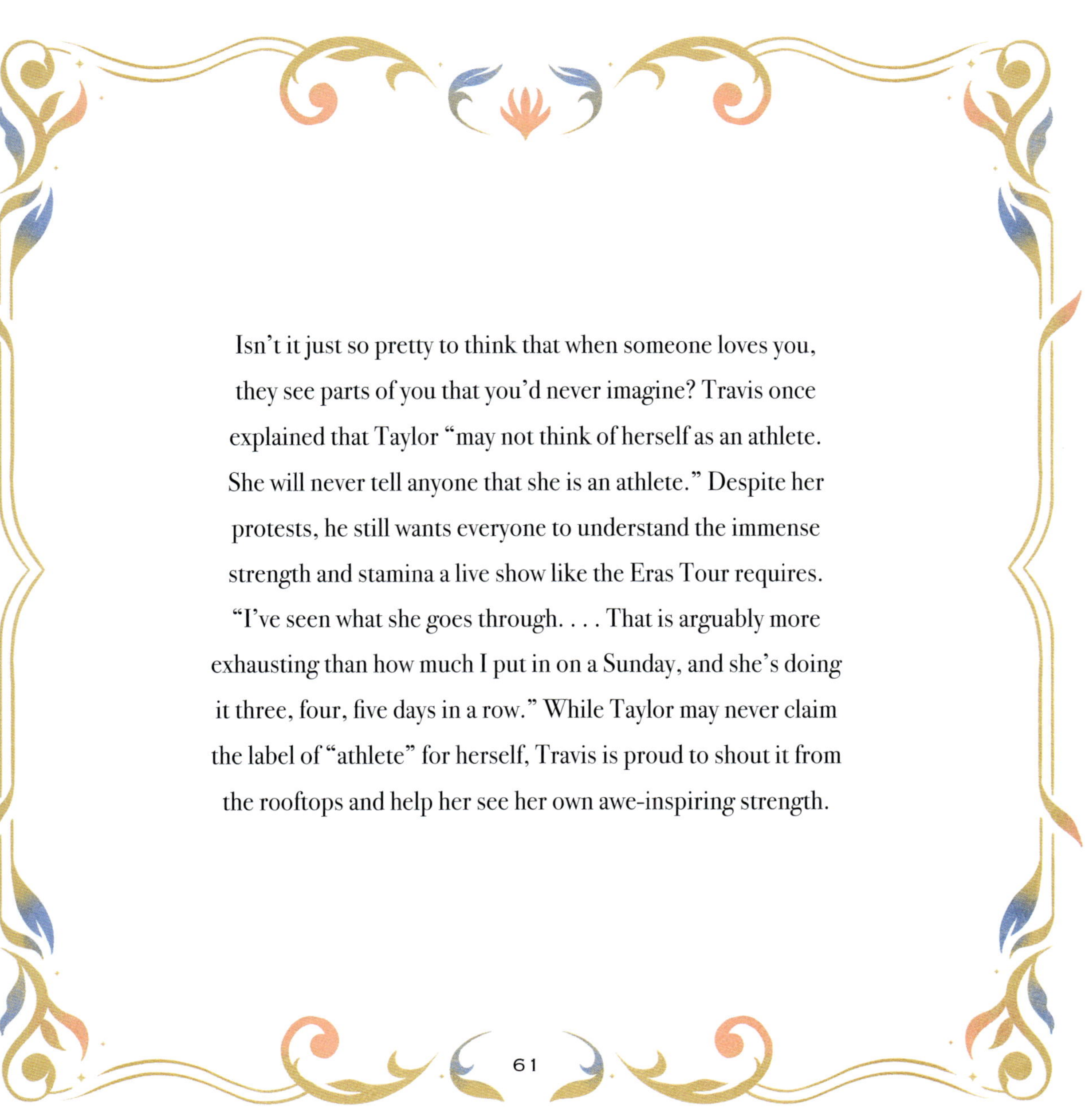

Isn't it just so pretty to think that when someone loves you, they see parts of you that you'd never imagine? Travis once explained that Taylor "may not think of herself as an athlete. She will never tell anyone that she is an athlete." Despite her protests, he still wants everyone to understand the immense strength and stamina a live show like the Eras Tour requires. "I've seen what she goes through. . . . That is arguably more exhausting than how much I put in on a Sunday, and she's doing it three, four, five days in a row." While Taylor may never claim the label of "athlete" for herself, Travis is proud to shout it from the rooftops and help her see her own awe-inspiring strength.

TRUE LOVE LOOKS FOR YOU IN THE CROWD.

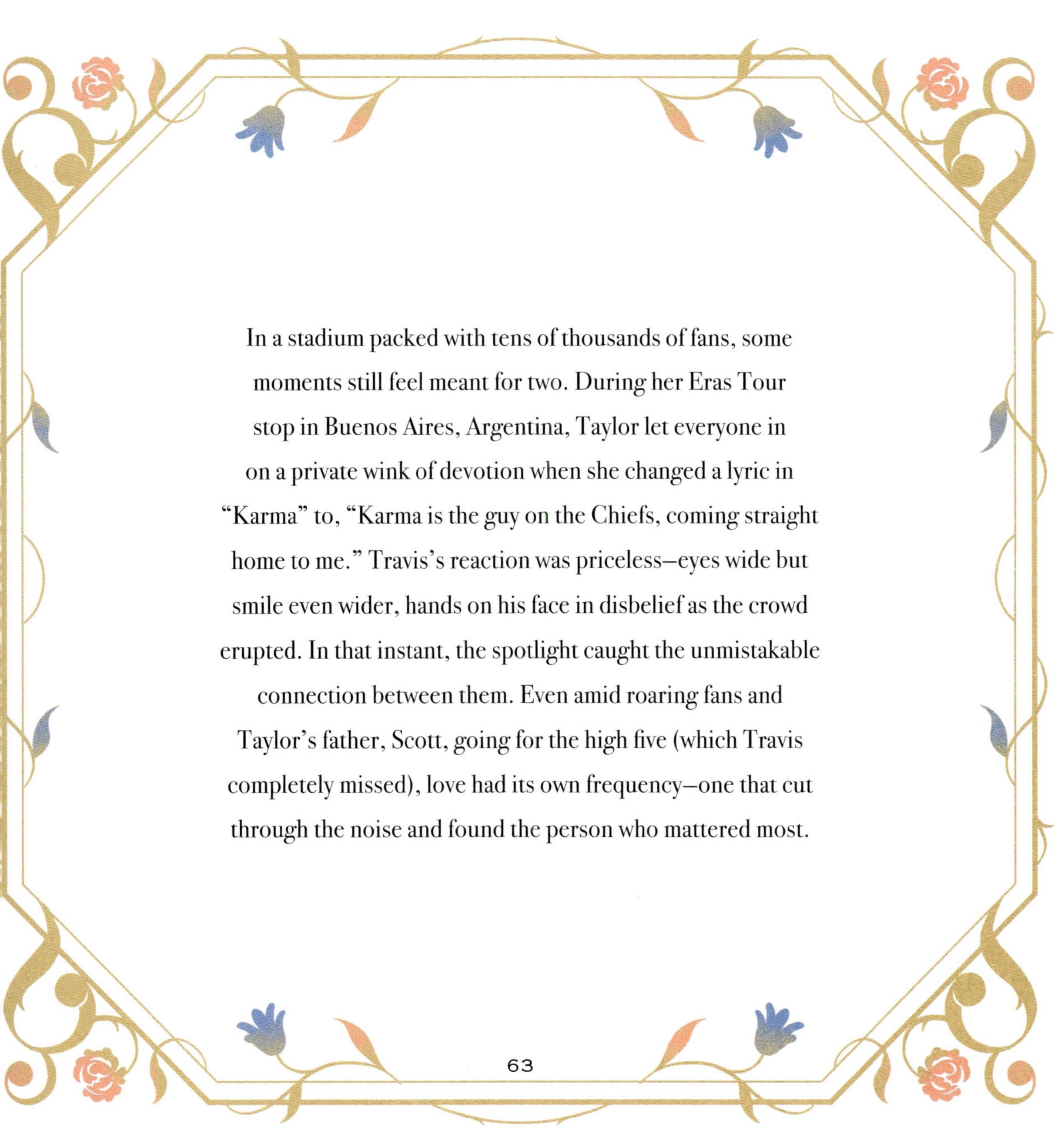

In a stadium packed with tens of thousands of fans, some moments still feel meant for two. During her Eras Tour stop in Buenos Aires, Argentina, Taylor let everyone in on a private wink of devotion when she changed a lyric in "Karma" to, "Karma is the guy on the Chiefs, coming straight home to me." Travis's reaction was priceless—eyes wide but smile even wider, hands on his face in disbelief as the crowd erupted. In that instant, the spotlight caught the unmistakable connection between them. Even amid roaring fans and Taylor's father, Scott, going for the high five (which Travis completely missed), love had its own frequency—one that cut through the noise and found the person who mattered most.

"He's all the things. He's, like, fun and vibrant and has this infectious personality. [He] makes me laugh so much."

—TAYLOR

"She is so good at mesmerizing everybody and making everybody feel like it's an intimate situation. . . . She's up there making everyone feel at ease."

—Travis

TRUE LOVE KNOWS YOUR WORTH AND ADDS INTEREST.

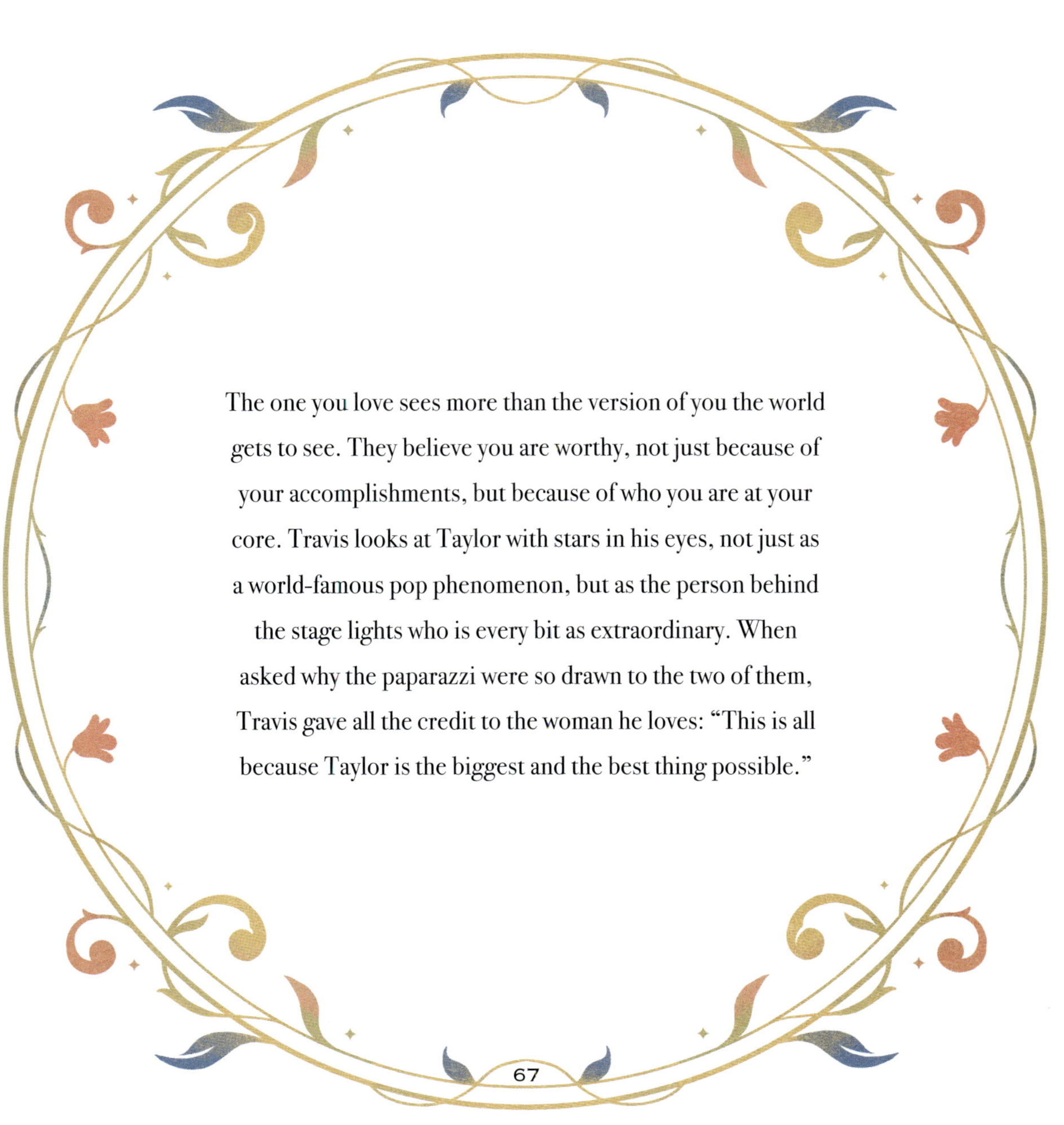

The one you love sees more than the version of you the world gets to see. They believe you are worthy, not just because of your accomplishments, but because of who you are at your core. Travis looks at Taylor with stars in his eyes, not just as a world-famous pop phenomenon, but as the person behind the stage lights who is every bit as extraordinary. When asked why the paparazzi were so drawn to the two of them, Travis gave all the credit to the woman he loves: "This is all because Taylor is the biggest and the best thing possible."

TRUE LOVE BECOMES FAMILY (CATS INCLUDED).

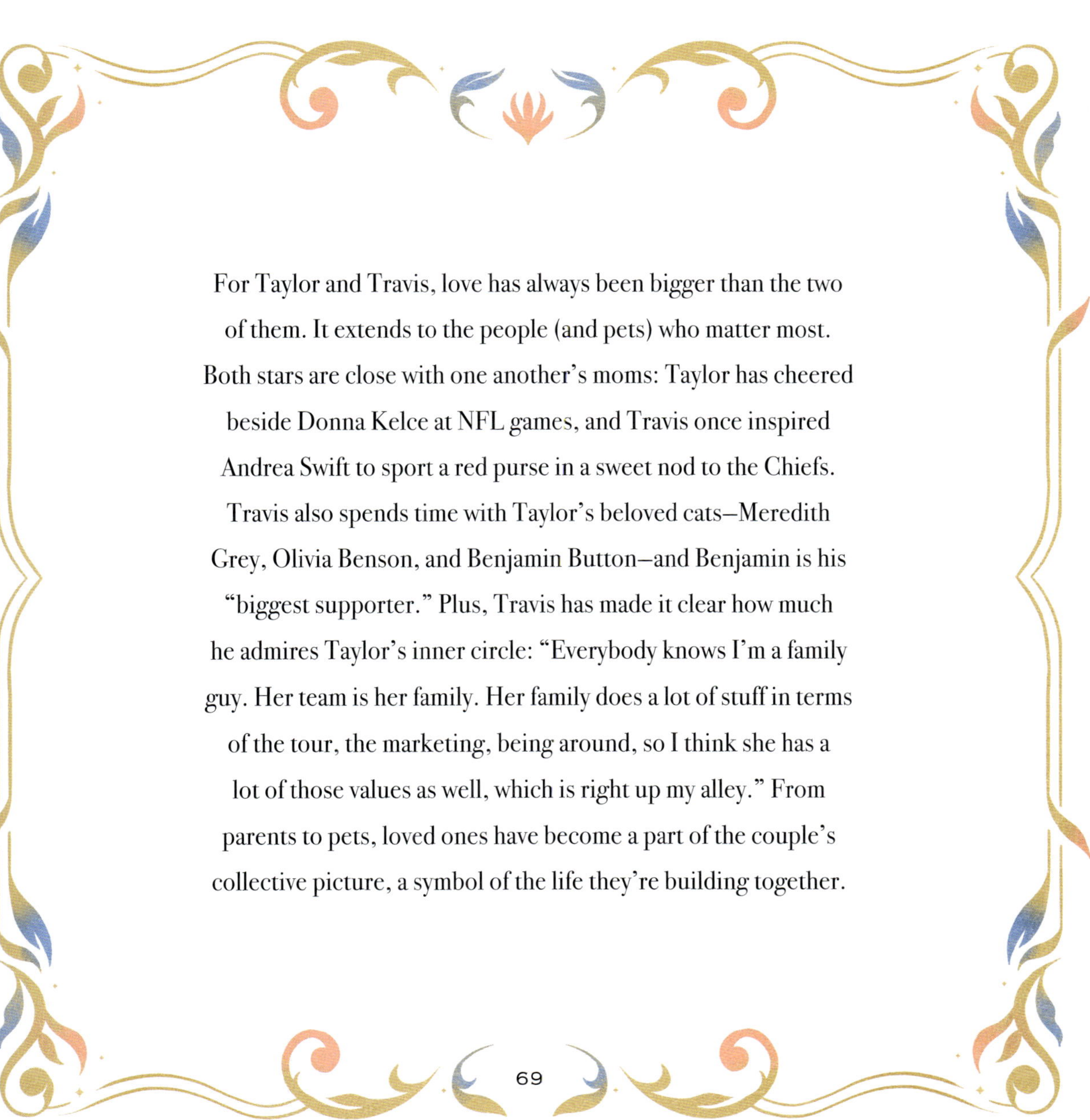

For Taylor and Travis, love has always been bigger than the two of them. It extends to the people (and pets) who matter most. Both stars are close with one another's moms: Taylor has cheered beside Donna Kelce at NFL games, and Travis once inspired Andrea Swift to sport a red purse in a sweet nod to the Chiefs. Travis also spends time with Taylor's beloved cats–Meredith Grey, Olivia Benson, and Benjamin Button–and Benjamin is his "biggest supporter." Plus, Travis has made it clear how much he admires Taylor's inner circle: "Everybody knows I'm a family guy. Her team is her family. Her family does a lot of stuff in terms of the tour, the marketing, being around, so I think she has a lot of those values as well, which is right up my alley." From parents to pets, loved ones have become a part of the couple's collective picture, a symbol of the life they're building together.

"My relatives, my cousins, were like, 'Please, please, please, he's amazing.' There were friends that were like, 'He's actually an amazing guy, he's so great.' There [were] a lot of people whispering in my ear about [him]."

—Taylor

"There were definitely people she knew that knew who I was, in her corner [who said]: 'Yo! Did you know he was coming?' I had somebody playing Cupid."

—Travis

TRUE LOVE FEELS LIKE HOME.

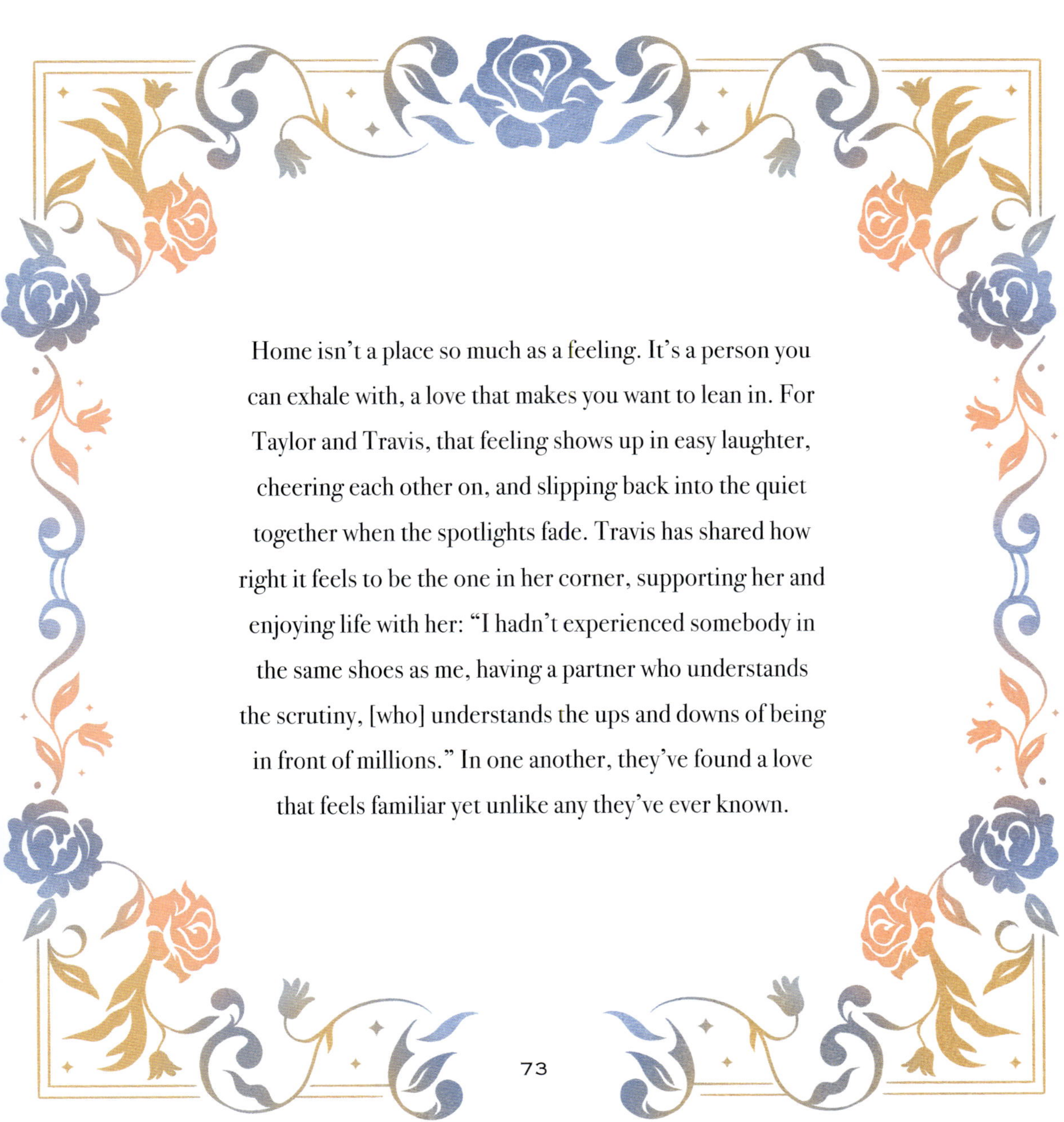

Home isn't a place so much as a feeling. It's a person you can exhale with, a love that makes you want to lean in. For Taylor and Travis, that feeling shows up in easy laughter, cheering each other on, and slipping back into the quiet together when the spotlights fade. Travis has shared how right it feels to be the one in her corner, supporting her and enjoying life with her: "I hadn't experienced somebody in the same shoes as me, having a partner who understands the scrutiny, [who] understands the ups and downs of being in front of millions." In one another, they've found a love that feels familiar yet unlike any they've ever known.

TRUE LOVE FILLS YOU UP.

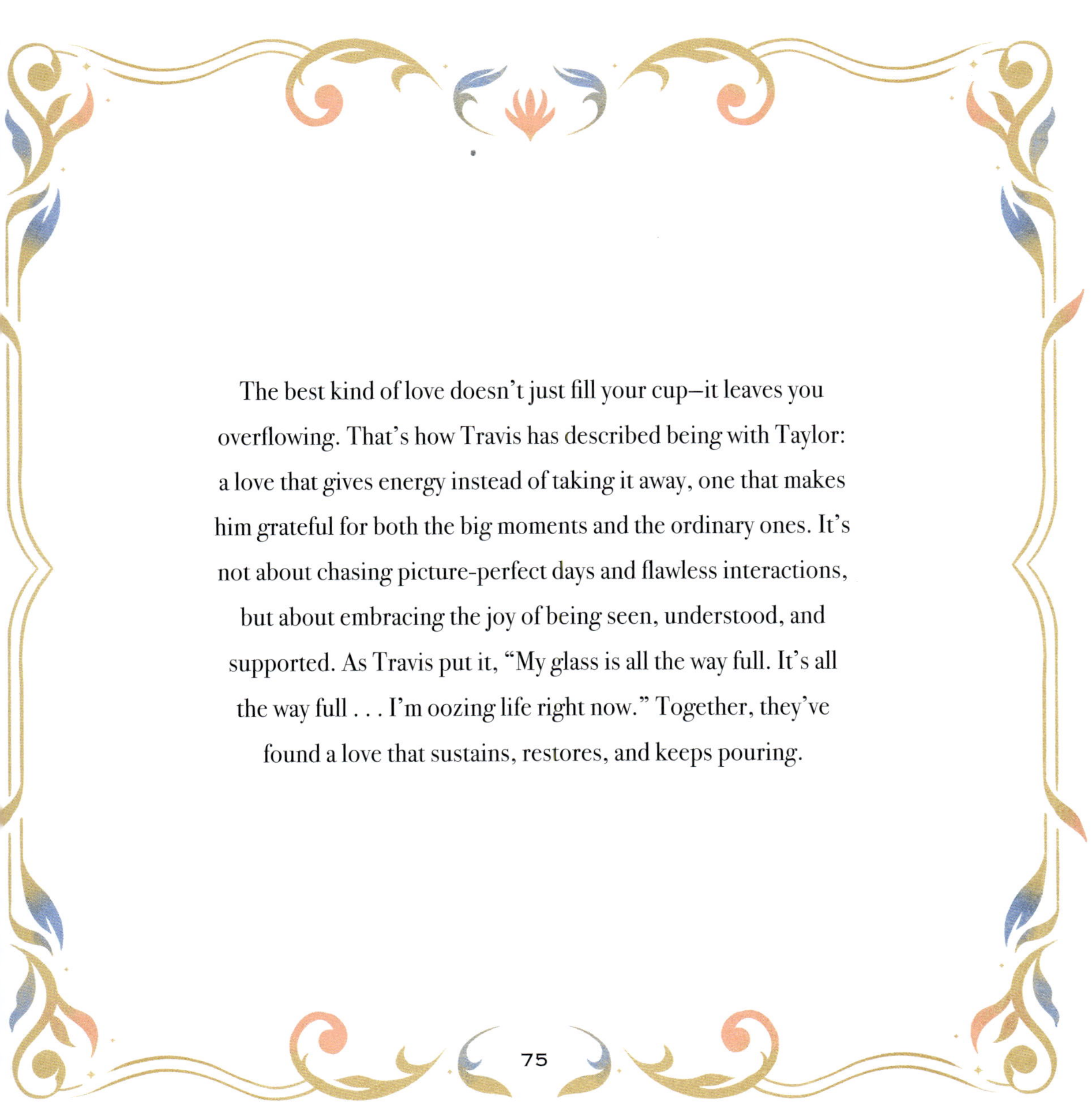

The best kind of love doesn't just fill your cup—it leaves you overflowing. That's how Travis has described being with Taylor: a love that gives energy instead of taking it away, one that makes him grateful for both the big moments and the ordinary ones. It's not about chasing picture-perfect days and flawless interactions, but about embracing the joy of being seen, understood, and supported. As Travis put it, "My glass is all the way full. It's all the way full . . . I'm oozing life right now." Together, they've found a love that sustains, restores, and keeps pouring.

TRUE LOVE TOASTS TO THE VICTORY OF "US" ABOVE ALL.

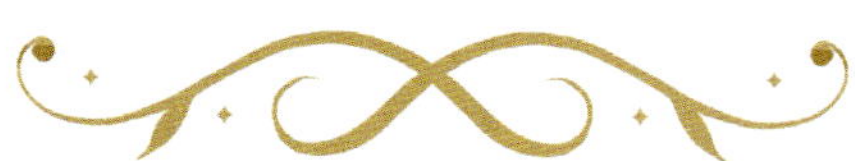

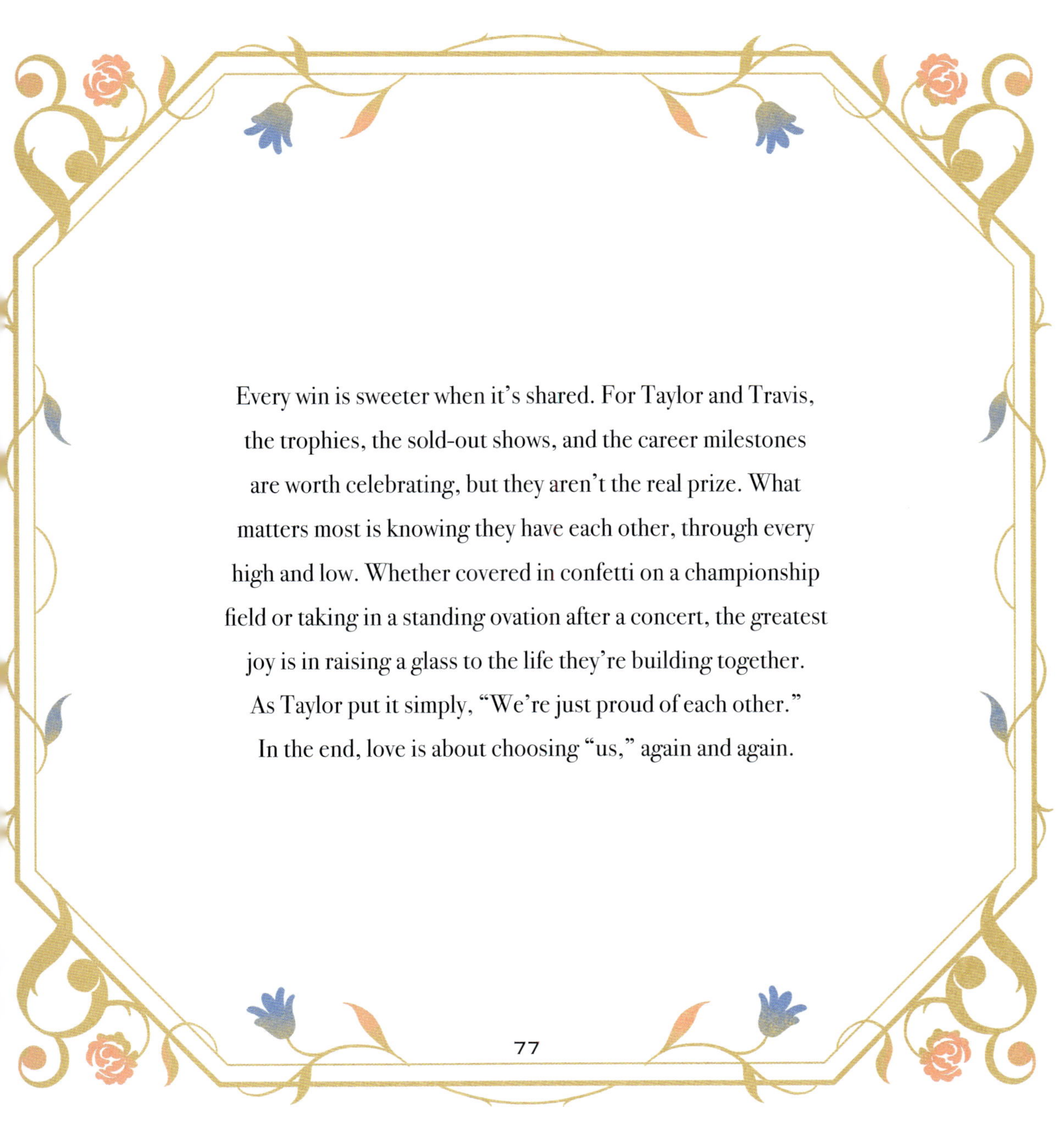

Every win is sweeter when it's shared. For Taylor and Travis, the trophies, the sold-out shows, and the career milestones are worth celebrating, but they aren't the real prize. What matters most is knowing they have each other, through every high and low. Whether covered in confetti on a championship field or taking in a standing ovation after a concert, the greatest joy is in raising a glass to the life they're building together. As Taylor put it simply, "We're just proud of each other." In the end, love is about choosing "us," again and again.

"I think we both love what we do and any chance that I can show my support to her—knowing that she has shown me all the support in the world throughout the season—it's just been an amazing experience getting to know Tay."

—Travis

"He's a blast. He's just the most fun person, the life of any party, even when it's just us. . . . That's the goal, isn't it? Find a best friend who you think is hot."

—TAYLOR

TRUE LOVE
LAUGHS
WITH YOU.

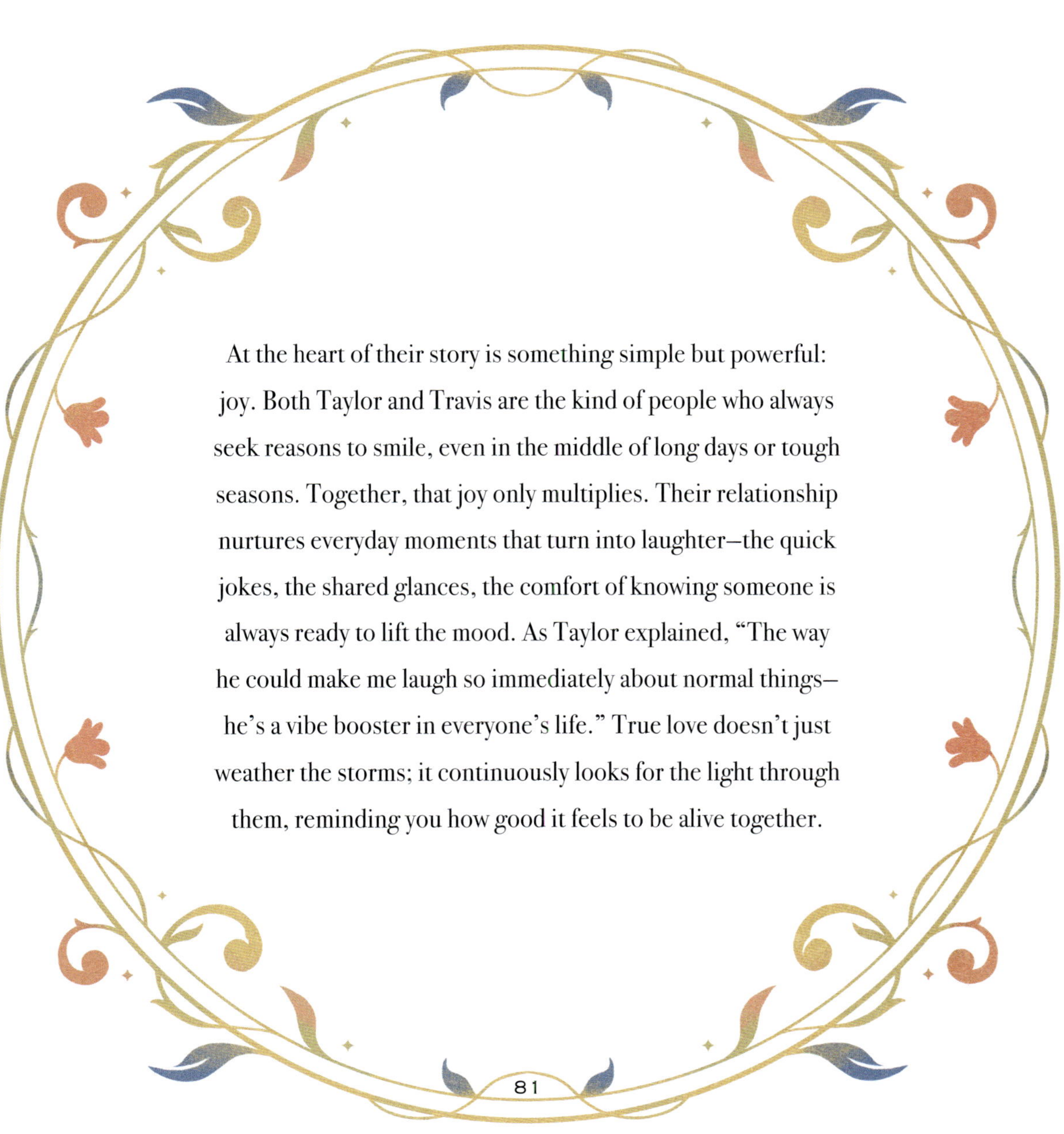

At the heart of their story is something simple but powerful: joy. Both Taylor and Travis are the kind of people who always seek reasons to smile, even in the middle of long days or tough seasons. Together, that joy only multiplies. Their relationship nurtures everyday moments that turn into laughter—the quick jokes, the shared glances, the comfort of knowing someone is always ready to lift the mood. As Taylor explained, "The way he could make me laugh so immediately about normal things—he's a vibe booster in everyone's life." True love doesn't just weather the storms; it continuously looks for the light through them, reminding you how good it feels to be alive together.

TRUE LOVE FEELS LIKE ANYTHING IS POSSIBLE.

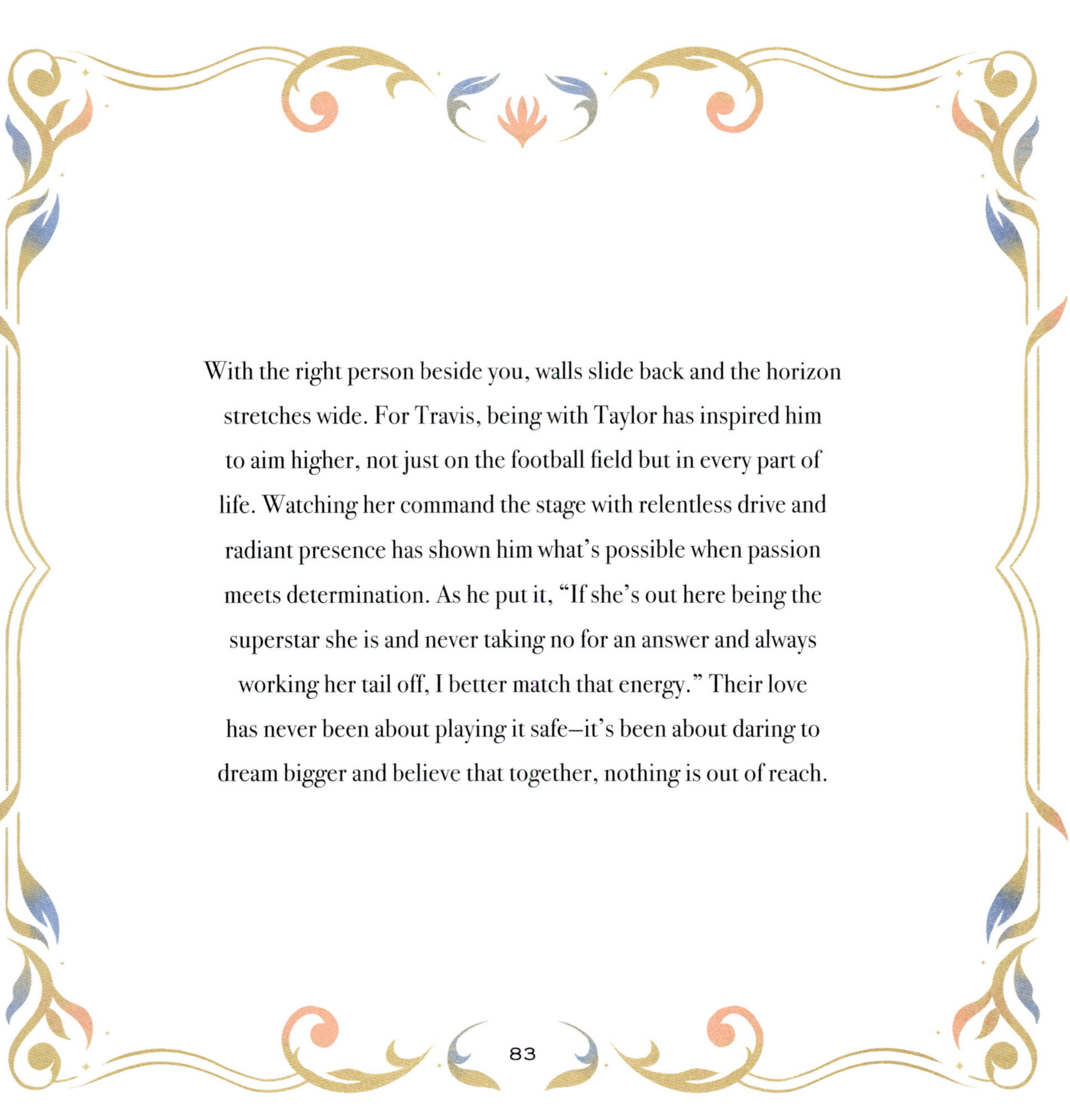

With the right person beside you, walls slide back and the horizon stretches wide. For Travis, being with Taylor has inspired him to aim higher, not just on the football field but in every part of life. Watching her command the stage with relentless drive and radiant presence has shown him what's possible when passion meets determination. As he put it, "If she's out here being the superstar she is and never taking no for an answer and always working her tail off, I better match that energy." Their love has never been about playing it safe–it's been about daring to dream bigger and believe that together, nothing is out of reach.

"[He's] just the warmest person. Depth without darkness."

—Taylor

"People gravitate toward how she performs and how she makes it feel like the entire stadium is in this little room with her."

—Travis

TRUE LOVE NEVER STOPS LEARNING.

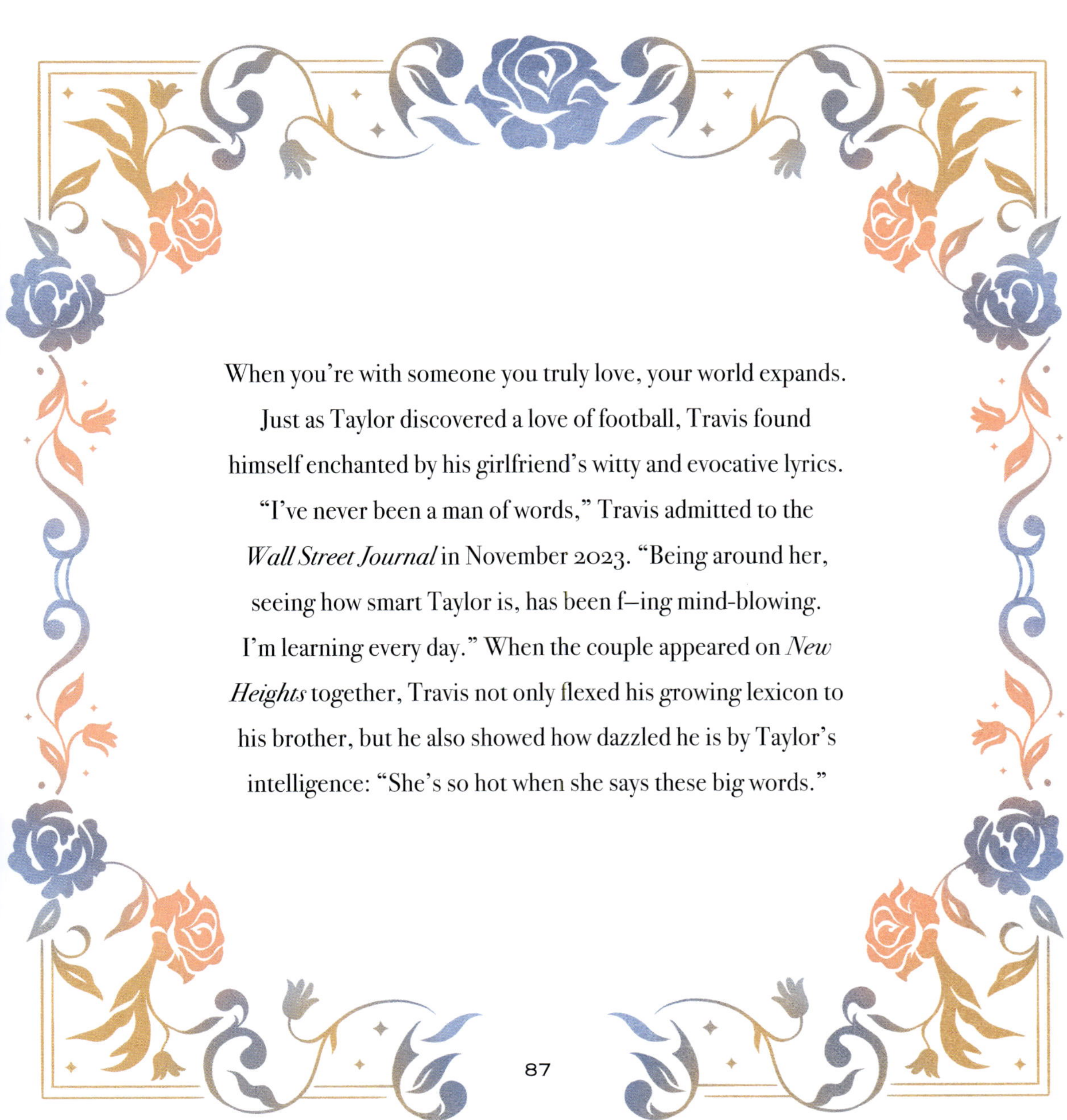

When you're with someone you truly love, your world expands. Just as Taylor discovered a love of football, Travis found himself enchanted by his girlfriend's witty and evocative lyrics. "I've never been a man of words," Travis admitted to the *Wall Street Journal* in November 2023. "Being around her, seeing how smart Taylor is, has been f—ing mind-blowing. I'm learning every day." When the couple appeared on *New Heights* together, Travis not only flexed his growing lexicon to his brother, but he also showed how dazzled he is by Taylor's intelligence: "She's so hot when she says these big words."

TRUE LOVE ADDS A LITTLE MAGIC TO EVERY DAY.

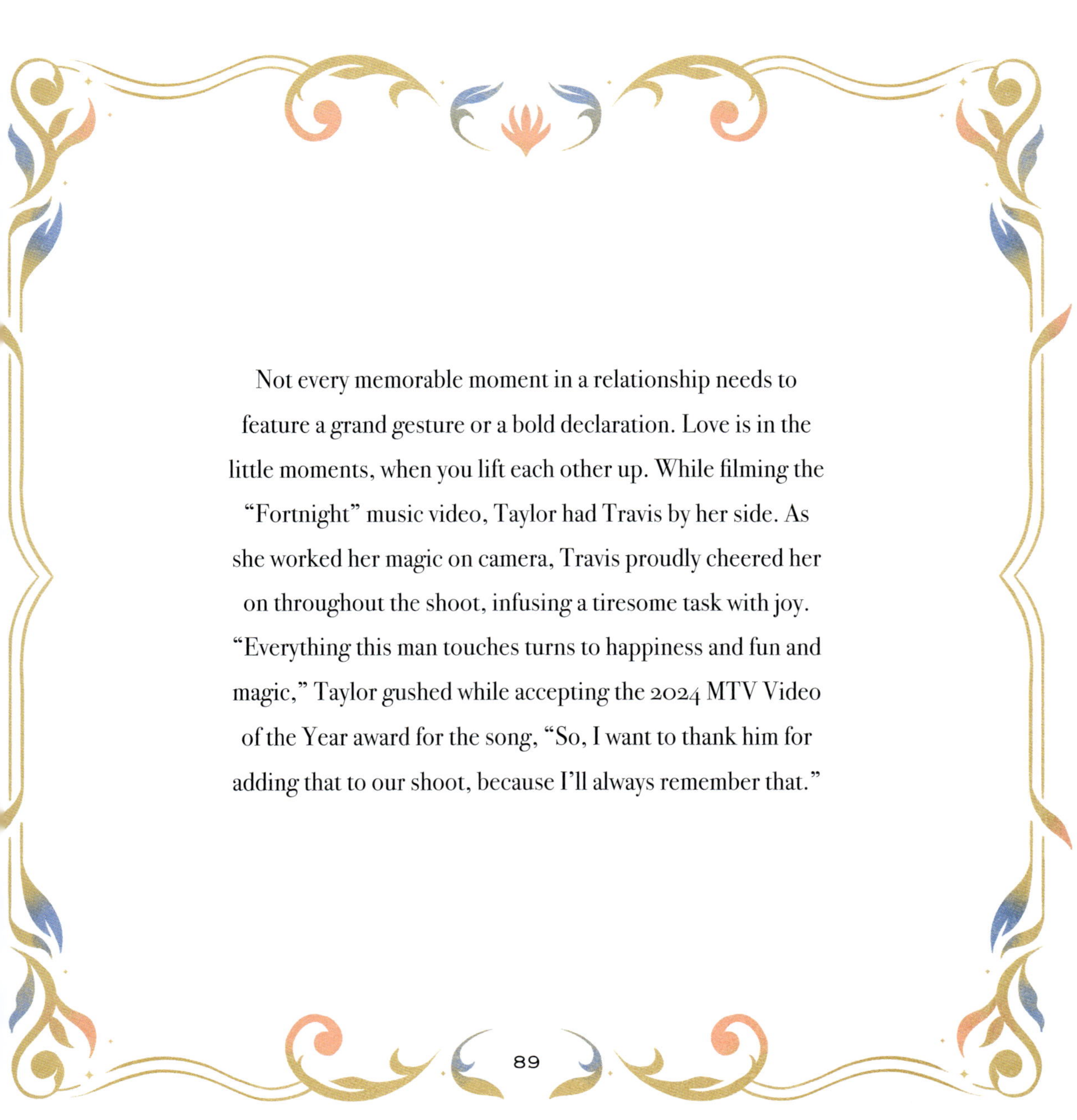

Not every memorable moment in a relationship needs to feature a grand gesture or a bold declaration. Love is in the little moments, when you lift each other up. While filming the "Fortnight" music video, Taylor had Travis by her side. As she worked her magic on camera, Travis proudly cheered her on throughout the shoot, infusing a tiresome task with joy. "Everything this man touches turns to happiness and fun and magic," Taylor gushed while accepting the 2024 MTV Video of the Year award for the song, "So, I want to thank him for adding that to our shoot, because I'll always remember that."

TRUE LOVE IS YOUR GOOD LUCK CHARM.

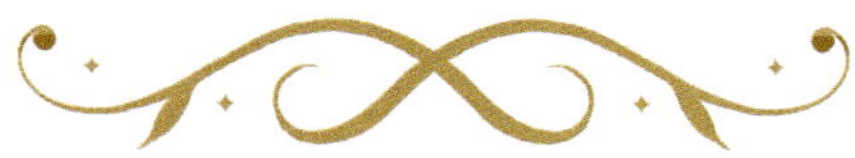

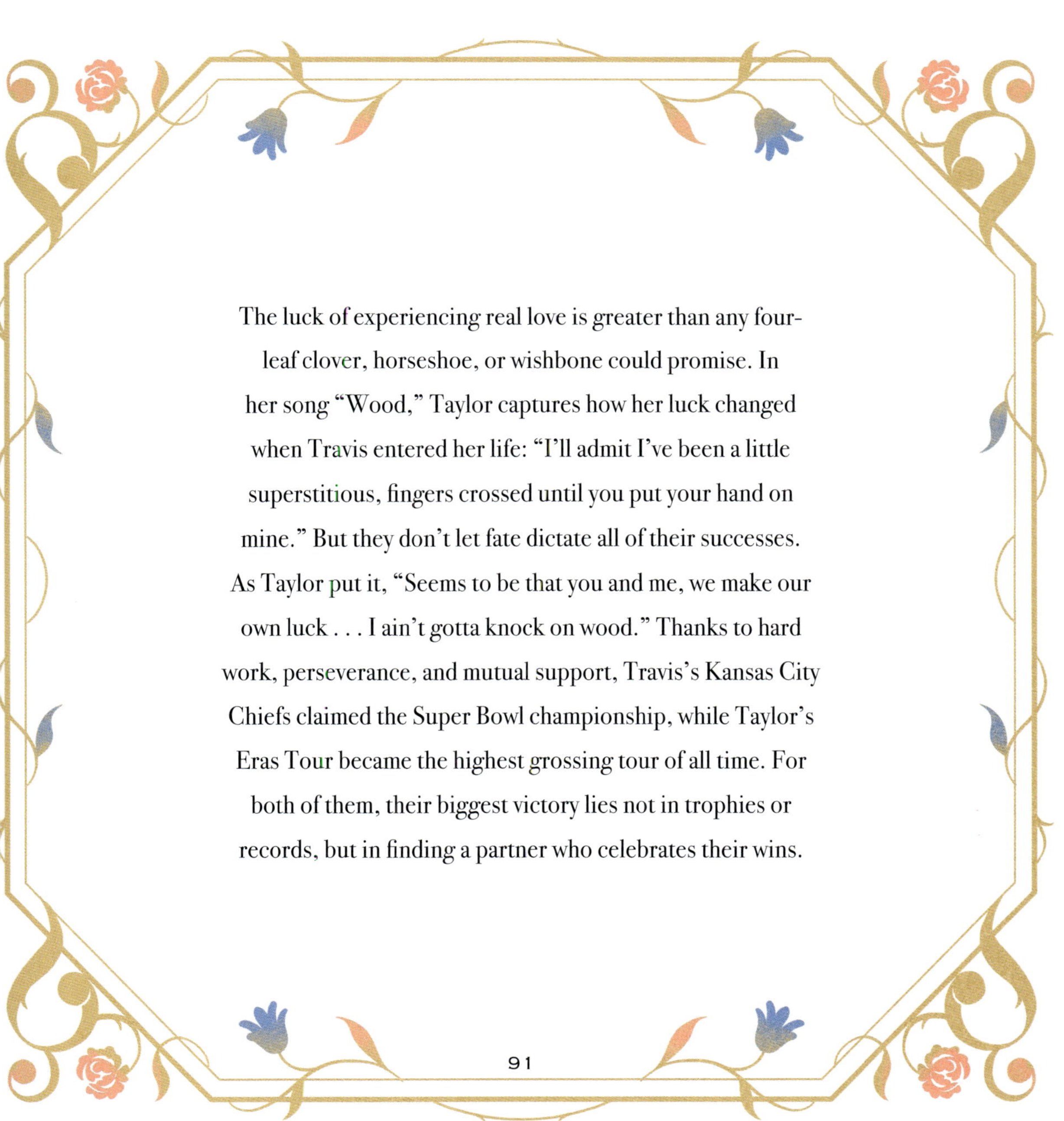

The luck of experiencing real love is greater than any four-leaf clover, horseshoe, or wishbone could promise. In her song "Wood," Taylor captures how her luck changed when Travis entered her life: "I'll admit I've been a little superstitious, fingers crossed until you put your hand on mine." But they don't let fate dictate all of their successes. As Taylor put it, "Seems to be that you and me, we make our own luck . . . I ain't gotta knock on wood." Thanks to hard work, perseverance, and mutual support, Travis's Kansas City Chiefs claimed the Super Bowl championship, while Taylor's Eras Tour became the highest grossing tour of all time. For both of them, their biggest victory lies not in trophies or records, but in finding a partner who celebrates their wins.

"People who fuel you, they fuel every part of you, and they make you walk taller, and they make you present in a more vibrant way."

—TAYLOR

"She loves coming to Arrowhead and coming to the games and cheering for me, so I got all the support in the world to keep chasing these dreams."

—Travis

TRUE LOVE IS SWEETER THAN FICTION.

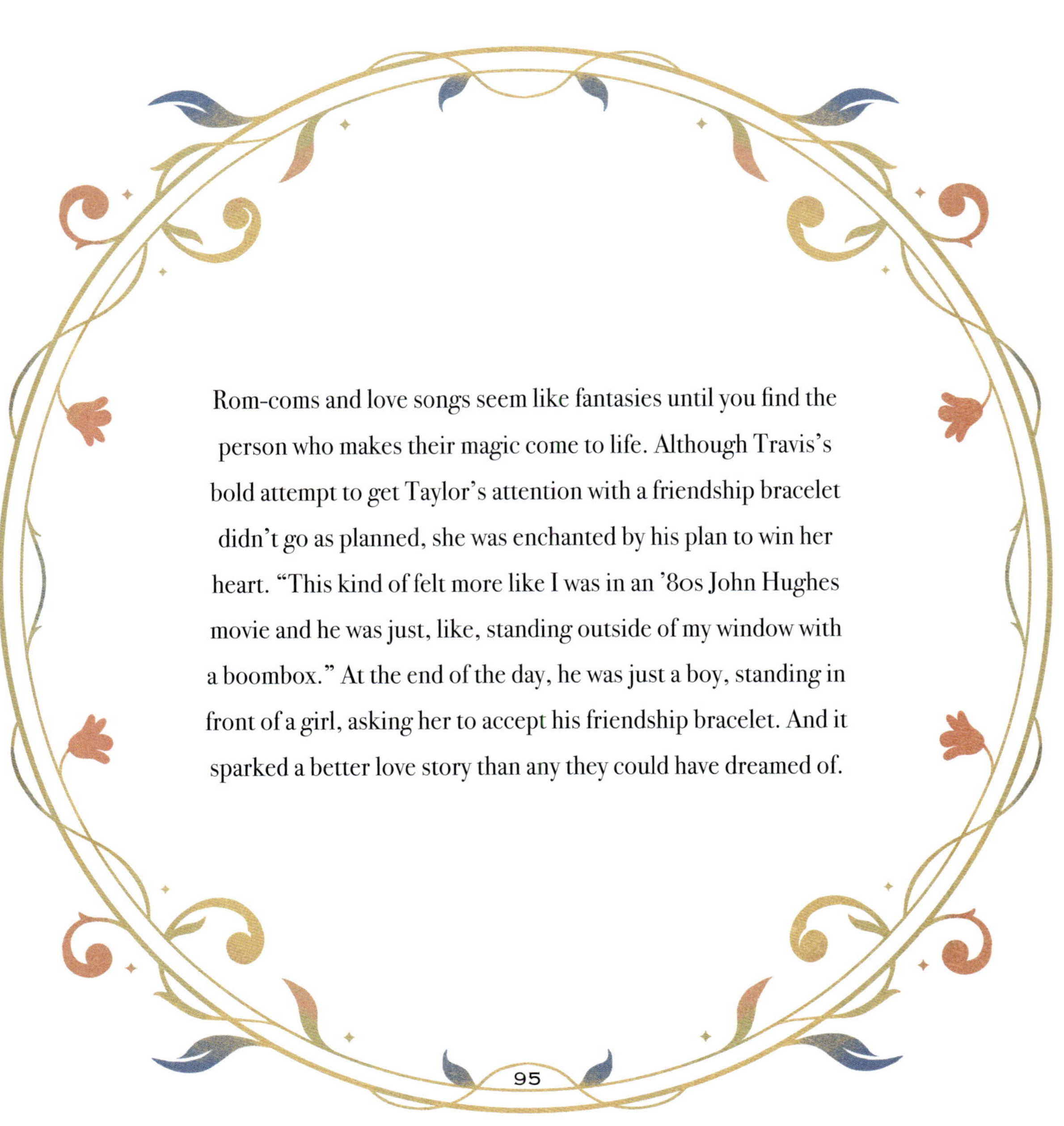

Rom-coms and love songs seem like fantasies until you find the person who makes their magic come to life. Although Travis's bold attempt to get Taylor's attention with a friendship bracelet didn't go as planned, she was enchanted by his plan to win her heart. "This kind of felt more like I was in an '80s John Hughes movie and he was just, like, standing outside of my window with a boombox." At the end of the day, he was just a boy, standing in front of a girl, asking her to accept his friendship bracelet. And it sparked a better love story than any they could have dreamed of.

TRUE LOVE
LIVES BY THE
SAME COMPASS.

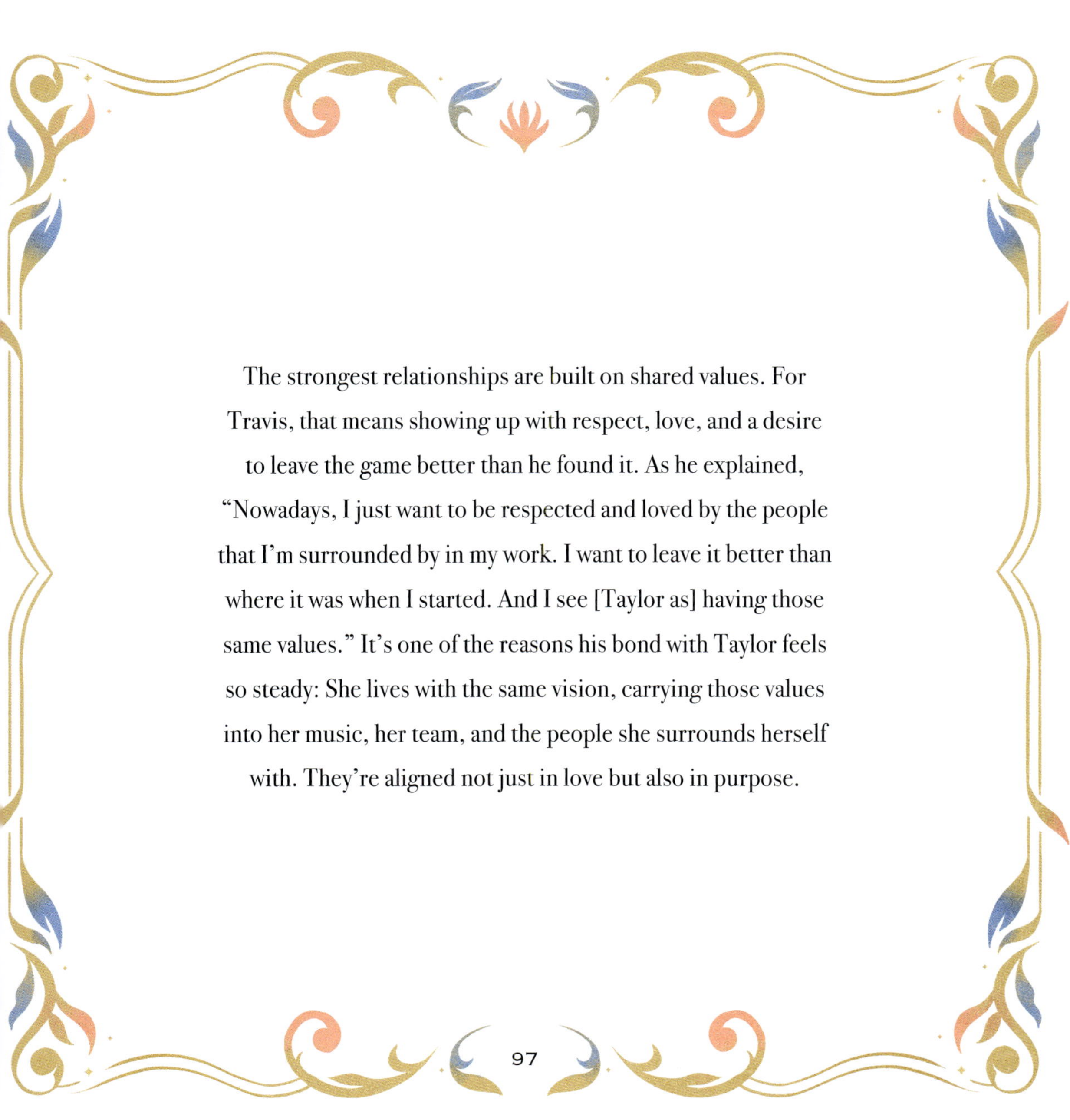

The strongest relationships are built on shared values. For Travis, that means showing up with respect, love, and a desire to leave the game better than he found it. As he explained, "Nowadays, I just want to be respected and loved by the people that I'm surrounded by in my work. I want to leave it better than where it was when I started. And I see [Taylor as] having those same values." It's one of the reasons his bond with Taylor feels so steady: She lives with the same vision, carrying those values into her music, her team, and the people she surrounds herself with. They're aligned not just in love but also in purpose.

"Everybody around me telling me, 'Don't f—k this up!' And me sitting here saying, 'Yeah—got it.' That was the biggest thing to me: Make sure I don't say anything that would push Taylor away."

—Travis

"A huge green flag is that Travis has had the same friends since he was probably four years old. . . . He's so loyal, and his friends are equally loyal, and they're just the funniest, most hilarious group of people."

—Taylor

TRUE LOVE DOESN'T PLAY GAMES.

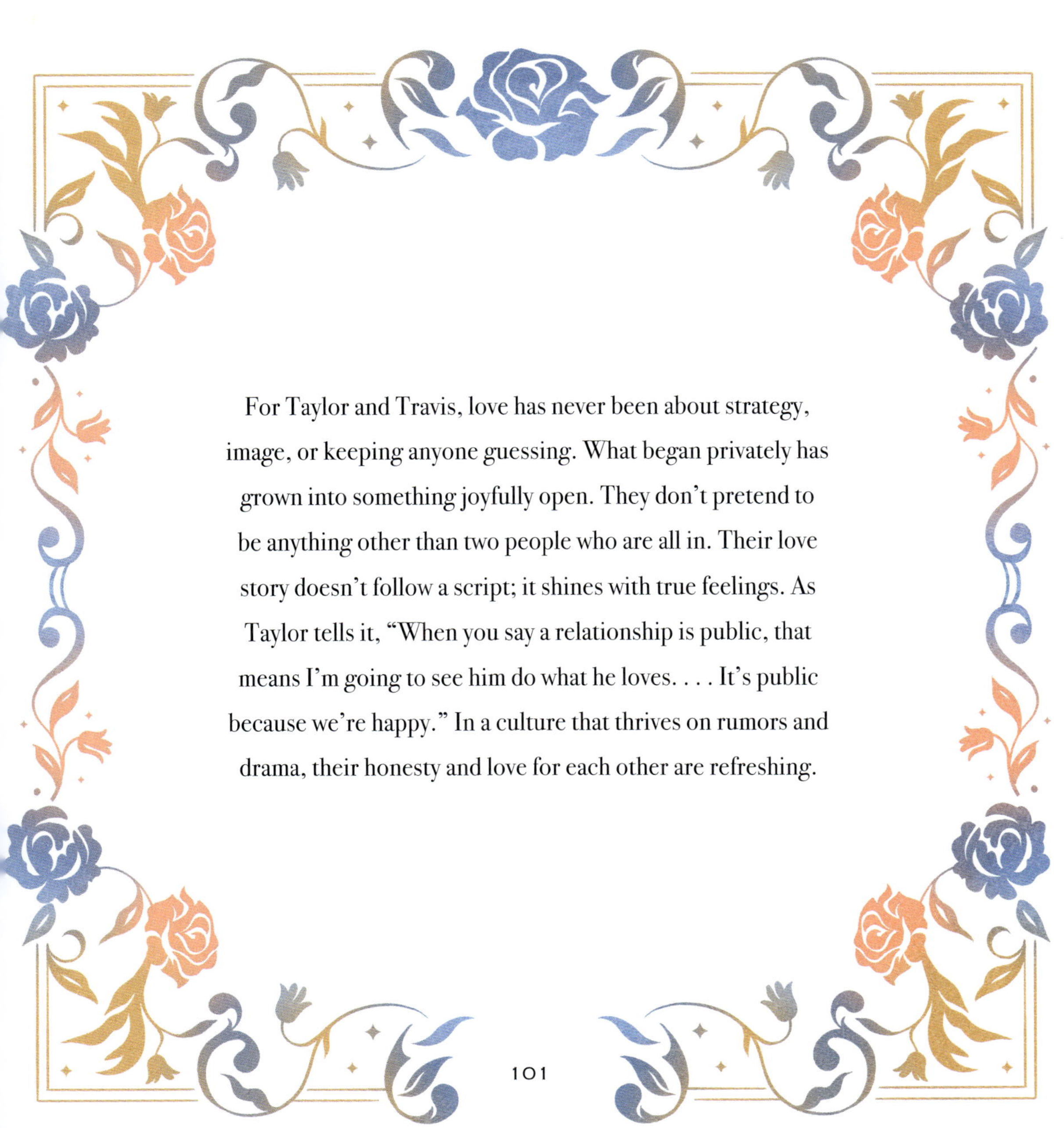

For Taylor and Travis, love has never been about strategy, image, or keeping anyone guessing. What began privately has grown into something joyfully open. They don't pretend to be anything other than two people who are all in. Their love story doesn't follow a script; it shines with true feelings. As Taylor tells it, "When you say a relationship is public, that means I'm going to see him do what he loves. . . . It's public because we're happy." In a culture that thrives on rumors and drama, their honesty and love for each other are refreshing.

TRUE LOVE
SPURS YOU ON.

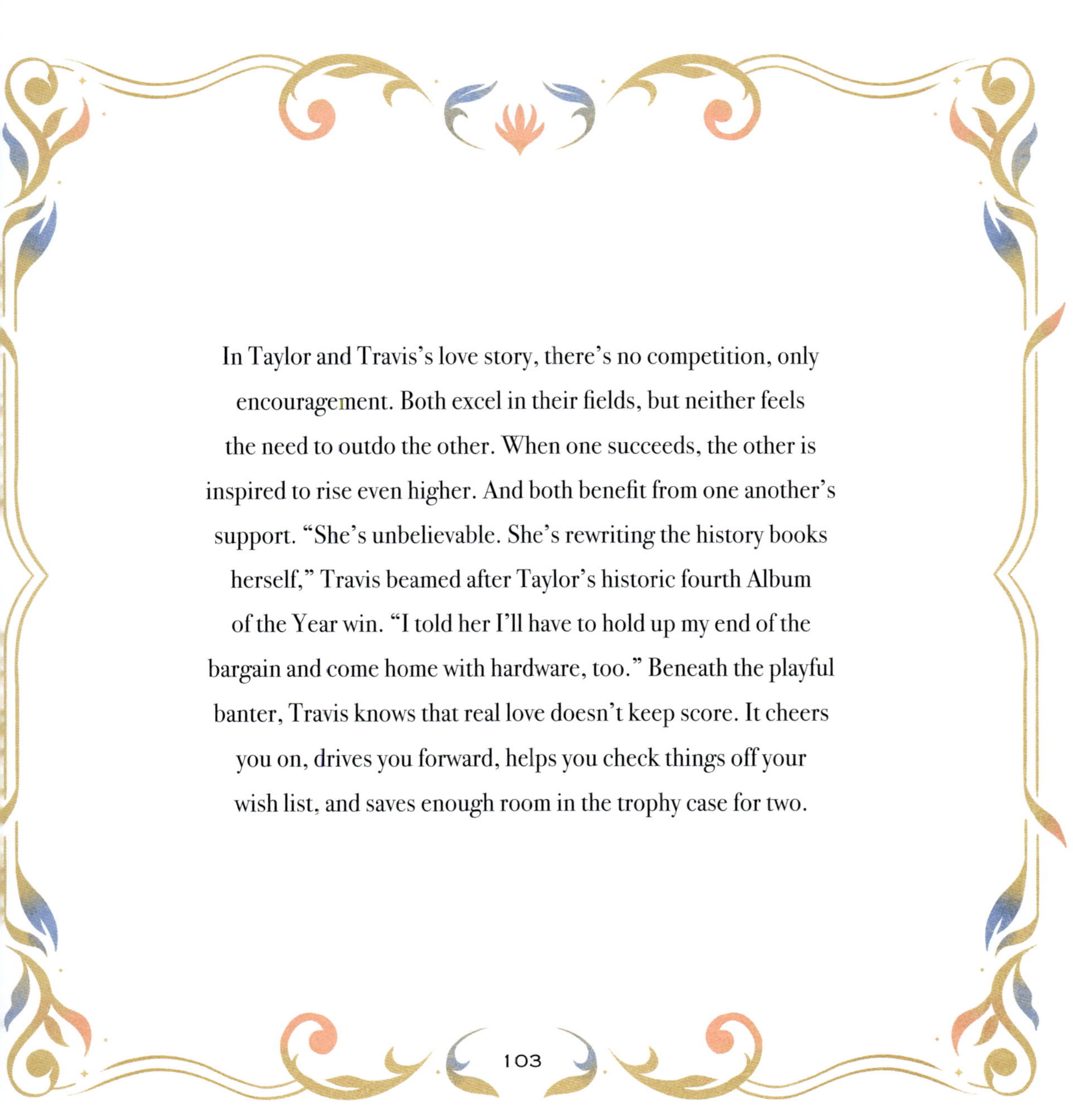

In Taylor and Travis's love story, there's no competition, only encouragement. Both excel in their fields, but neither feels the need to outdo the other. When one succeeds, the other is inspired to rise even higher. And both benefit from one another's support. "She's unbelievable. She's rewriting the history books herself," Travis beamed after Taylor's historic fourth Album of the Year win. "I told her I'll have to hold up my end of the bargain and come home with hardware, too." Beneath the playful banter, Travis knows that real love doesn't keep score. It cheers you on, drives you forward, helps you check things off your wish list, and saves enough room in the trophy case for two.

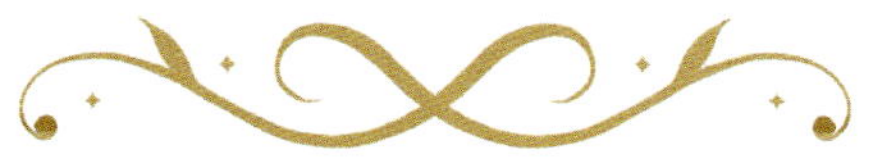

TRUE LOVE IS PROUD, NOT POSSESSIVE.

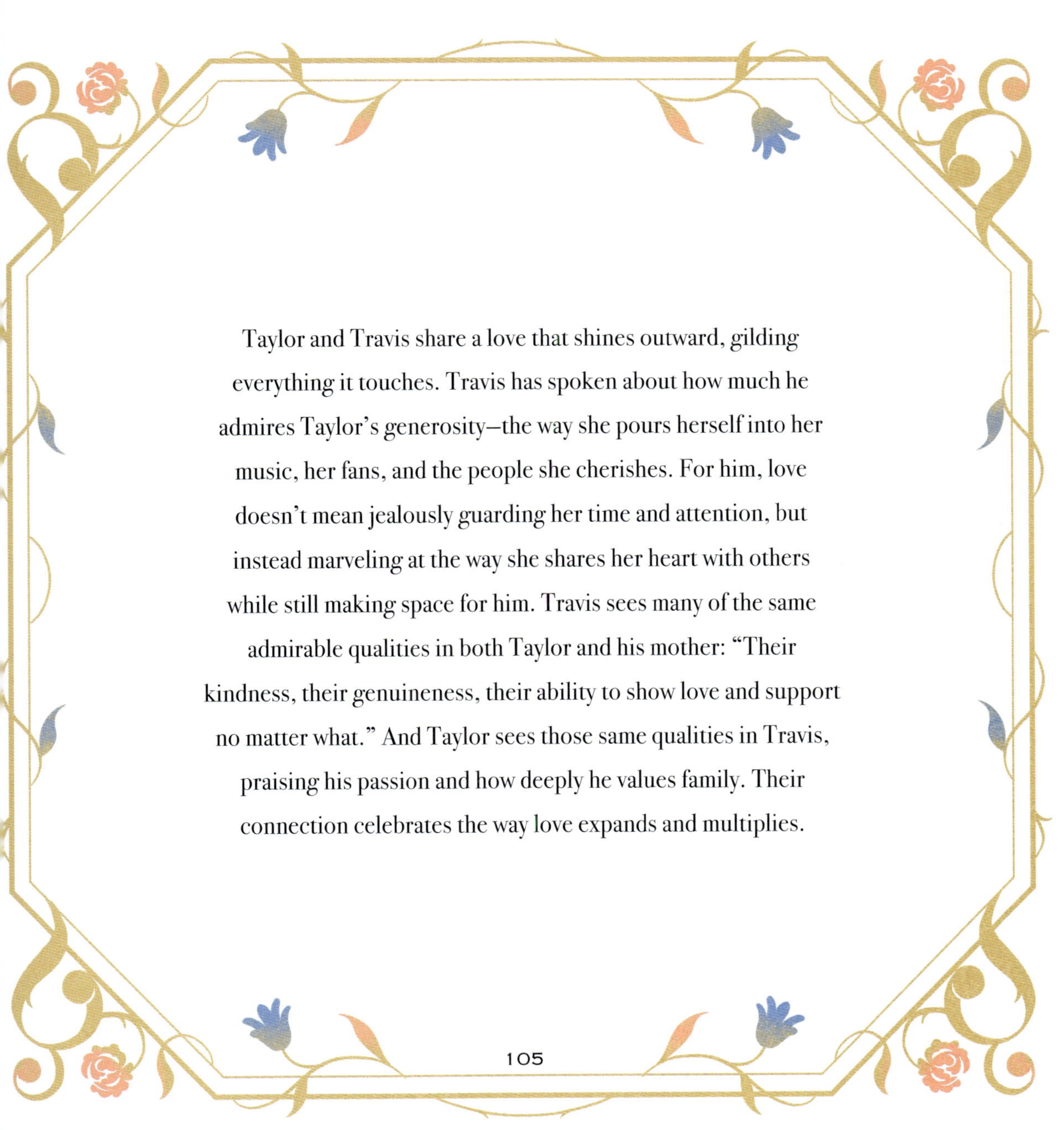

Taylor and Travis share a love that shines outward, gilding everything it touches. Travis has spoken about how much he admires Taylor's generosity–the way she pours herself into her music, her fans, and the people she cherishes. For him, love doesn't mean jealously guarding her time and attention, but instead marveling at the way she shares her heart with others while still making space for him. Travis sees many of the same admirable qualities in both Taylor and his mother: "Their kindness, their genuineness, their ability to show love and support no matter what." And Taylor sees those same qualities in Travis, praising his passion and how deeply he values family. Their connection celebrates the way love expands and multiplies.

"That's the thing with love: It's going to be wrong until it's right."

—Taylor

"I love being the happiest guy in the world all the f—ing time."

—Travis

TRUE LOVE
TURNS RAIN
INTO
RAINBOWS.

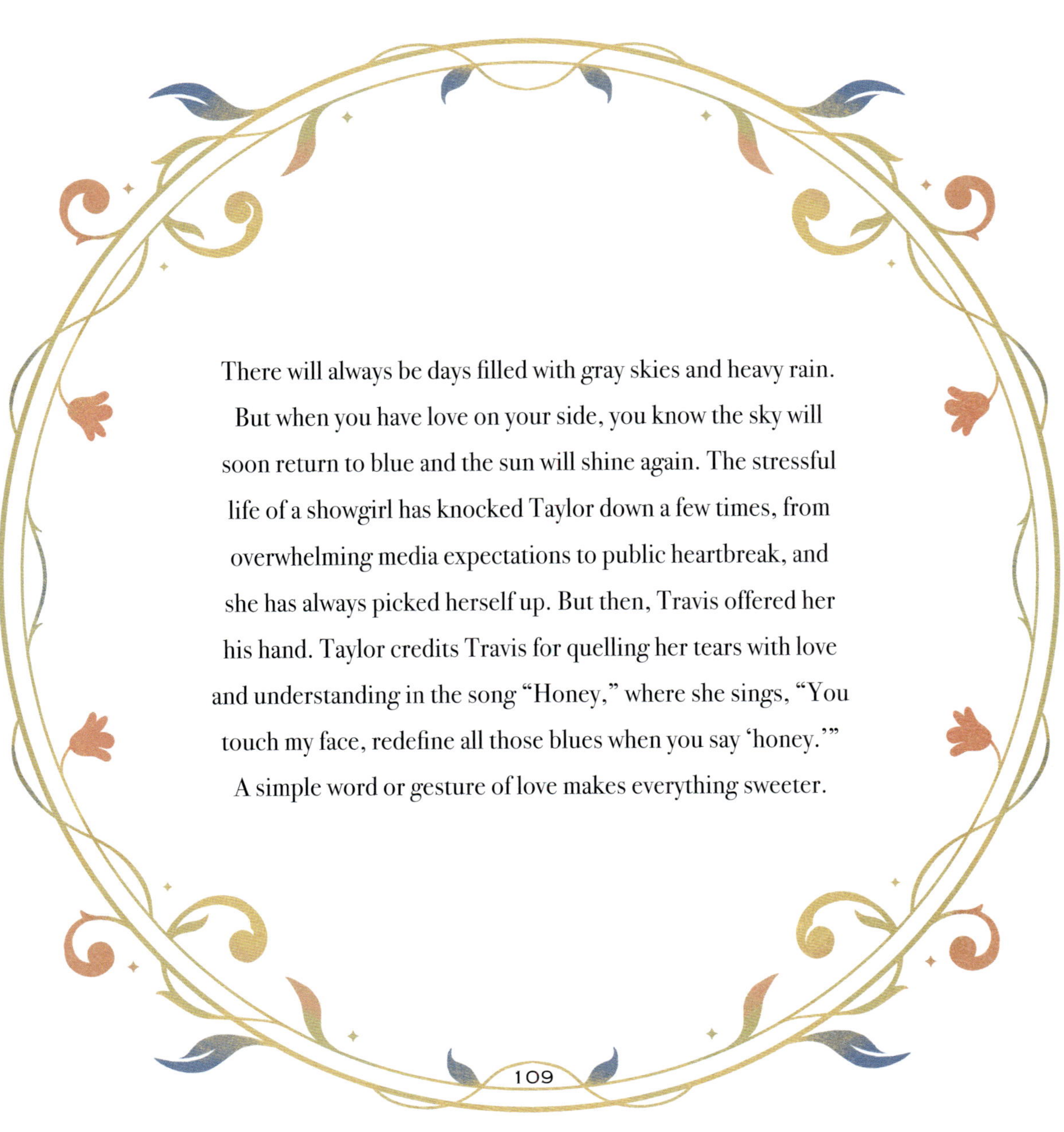

There will always be days filled with gray skies and heavy rain. But when you have love on your side, you know the sky will soon return to blue and the sun will shine again. The stressful life of a showgirl has knocked Taylor down a few times, from overwhelming media expectations to public heartbreak, and she has always picked herself up. But then, Travis offered her his hand. Taylor credits Travis for quelling her tears with love and understanding in the song "Honey," where she sings, "You touch my face, redefine all those blues when you say 'honey.'" A simple word or gesture of love makes everything sweeter.

TRUE LOVE
STANDS
BESIDE YOU IN
THE THICK OF IT.

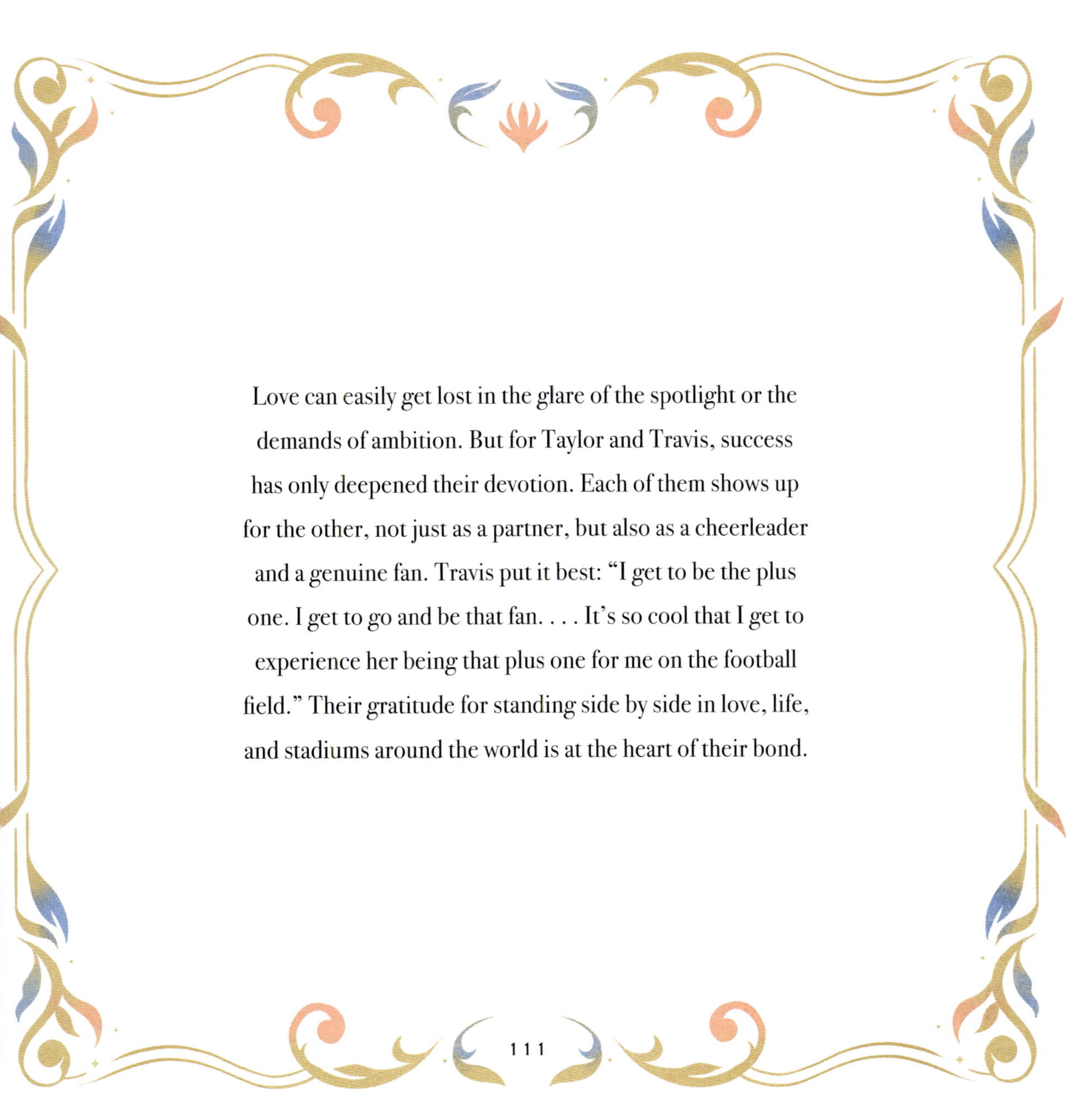

Love can easily get lost in the glare of the spotlight or the demands of ambition. But for Taylor and Travis, success has only deepened their devotion. Each of them shows up for the other, not just as a partner, but also as a cheerleader and a genuine fan. Travis put it best: "I get to be the plus one. I get to go and be that fan. . . . It's so cool that I get to experience her being that plus one for me on the football field." Their gratitude for standing side by side in love, life, and stadiums around the world is at the heart of their bond.

"He really crushed it when it came to surprising me...behind his house, he was having the whole back garden turned into this [proposal setting]."

—TAYLOR

"I'm an emotional guy, so there were a few tears here and there, but it's been an exciting ride up to this day."

—Travis

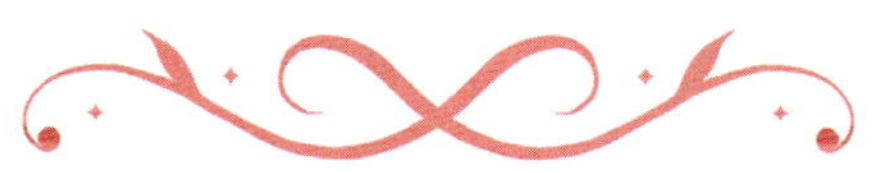

TRUE LOVE
LEAVES NOTHING
ON THE TABLE.

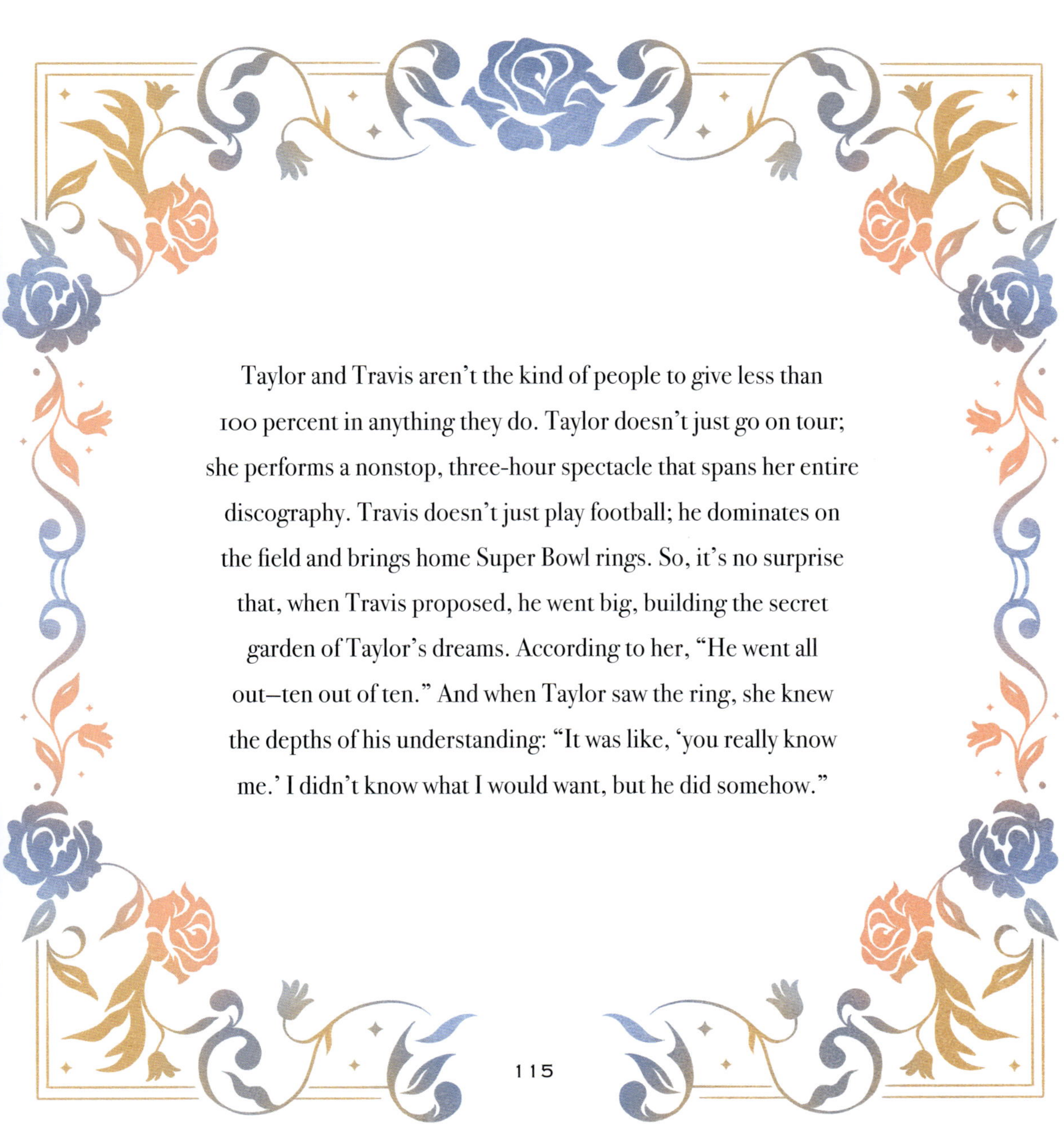

Taylor and Travis aren't the kind of people to give less than 100 percent in anything they do. Taylor doesn't just go on tour; she performs a nonstop, three-hour spectacle that spans her entire discography. Travis doesn't just play football; he dominates on the field and brings home Super Bowl rings. So, it's no surprise that, when Travis proposed, he went big, building the secret garden of Taylor's dreams. According to her, "He went all out–ten out of ten." And when Taylor saw the ring, she knew the depths of his understanding: "It was like, 'you really know me.' I didn't know what I would want, but he did somehow."

TRUE LOVE
GROUNDS YOU.

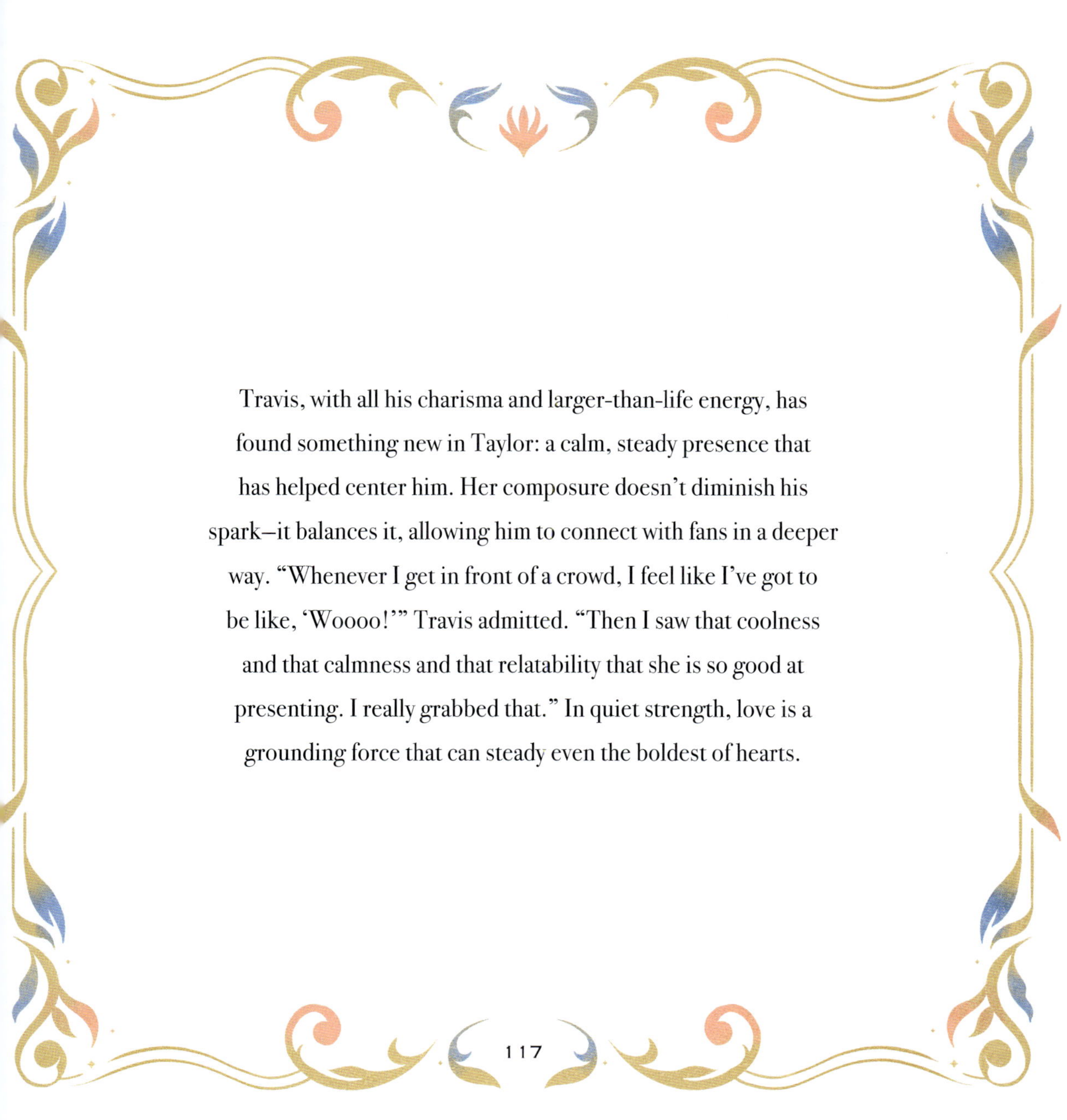

Travis, with all his charisma and larger-than-life energy, has found something new in Taylor: a calm, steady presence that has helped center him. Her composure doesn't diminish his spark–it balances it, allowing him to connect with fans in a deeper way. "Whenever I get in front of a crowd, I feel like I've got to be like, 'Woooo!'" Travis admitted. "Then I saw that coolness and that calmness and that relatability that she is so good at presenting. I really grabbed that." In quiet strength, love is a grounding force that can steady even the boldest of hearts.

TRUE LOVE
BRIDGES
DIVIDES.

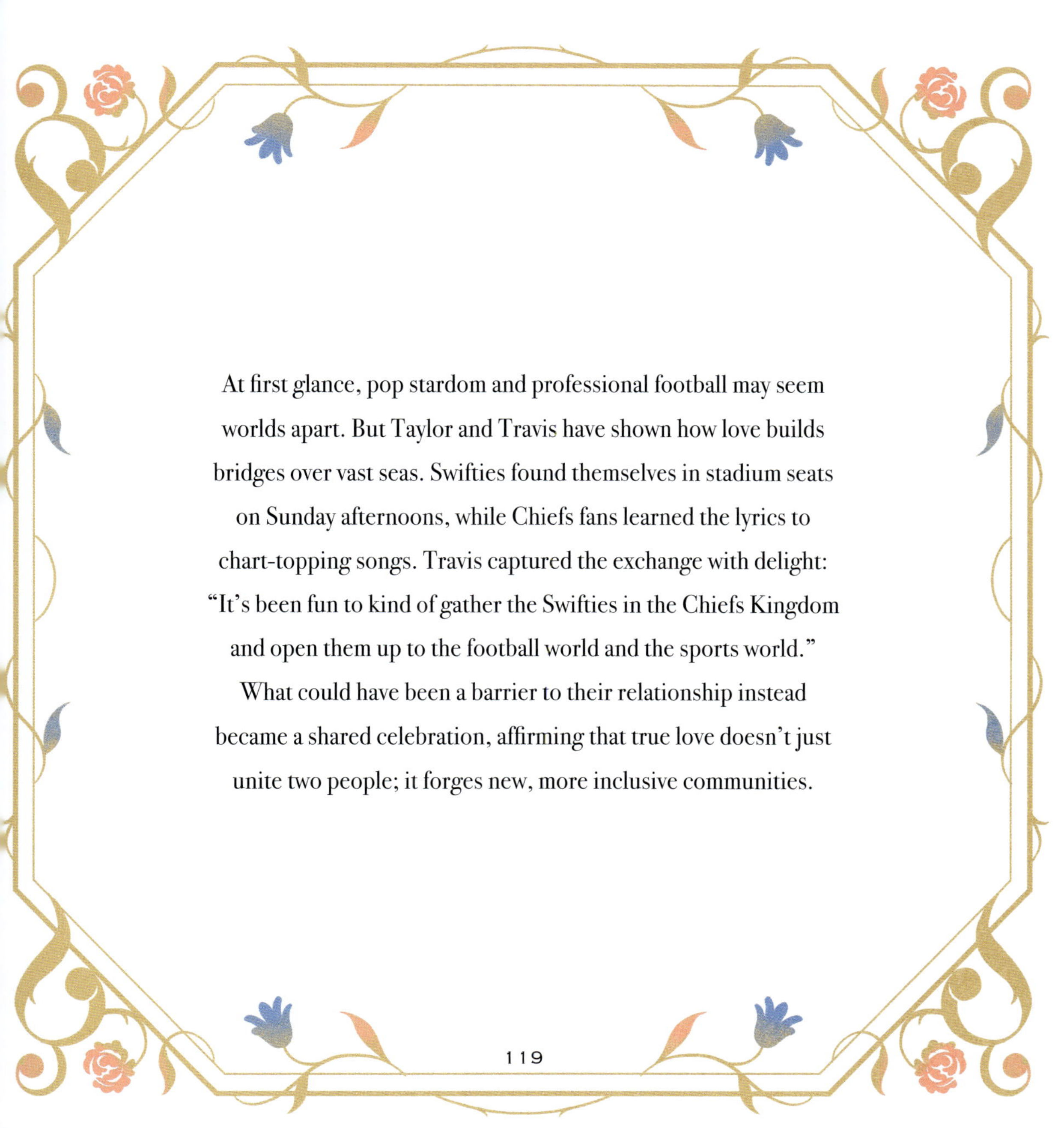

At first glance, pop stardom and professional football may seem worlds apart. But Taylor and Travis have shown how love builds bridges over vast seas. Swifties found themselves in stadium seats on Sunday afternoons, while Chiefs fans learned the lyrics to chart-topping songs. Travis captured the exchange with delight: “It’s been fun to kind of gather the Swifties in the Chiefs Kingdom and open them up to the football world and the sports world.” What could have been a barrier to their relationship instead became a shared celebration, affirming that true love doesn’t just unite two people; it forges new, more inclusive communities.

"If I would have never gone to that show and been mesmerized and just been captivated, and then left with such a desire to want to meet [her], I would have never went on here and told everybody how butthurt I was."

—Travis

"I owe a lot to [New Heights]. This podcast got me a boyfriend ever since Travis decided to use it as his personal dating app."

—Taylor

TRUE LOVE IS EVERYTHING YOU'VE WISHED FOR.

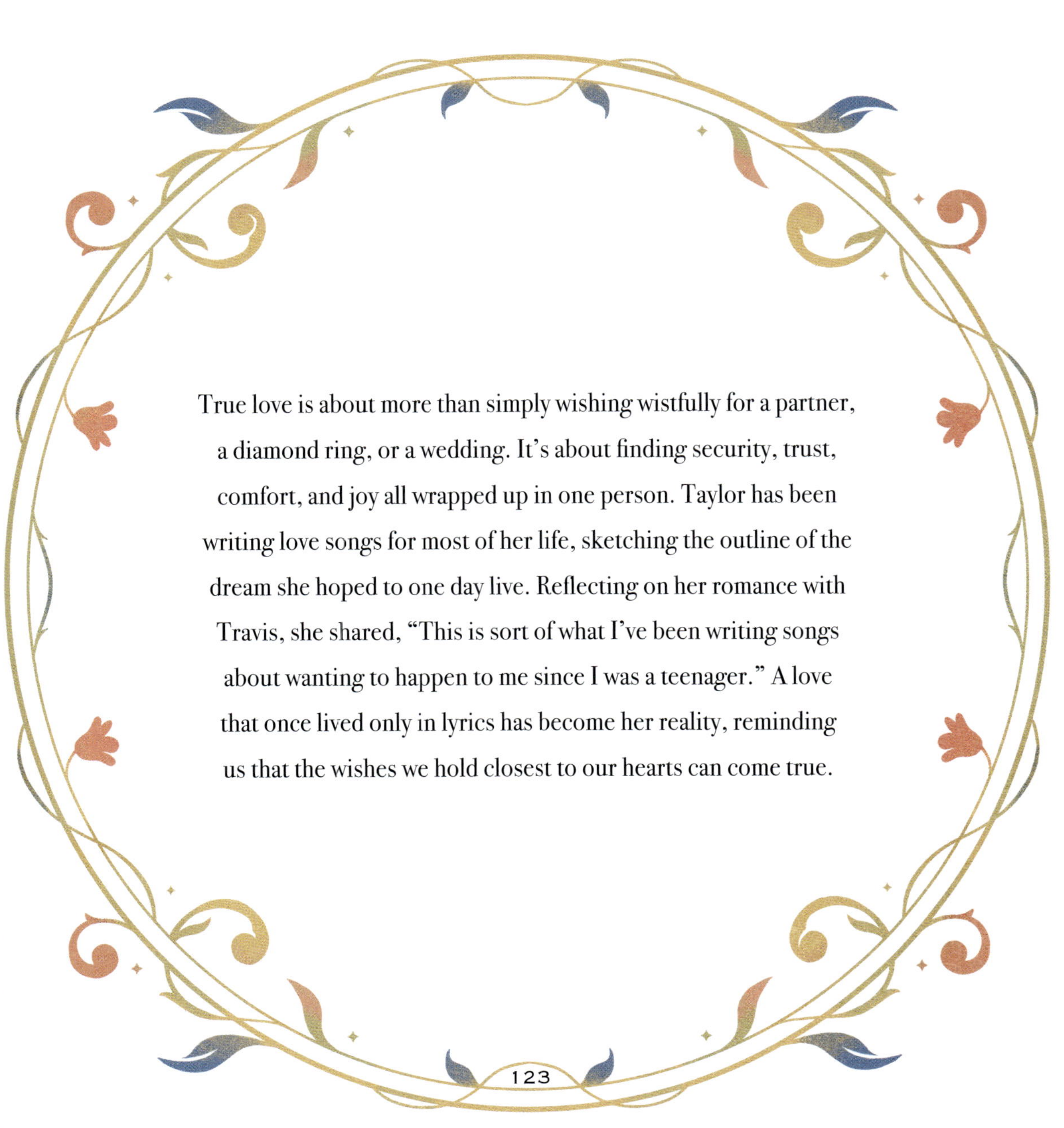

True love is about more than simply wishing wistfully for a partner, a diamond ring, or a wedding. It's about finding security, trust, comfort, and joy all wrapped up in one person. Taylor has been writing love songs for most of her life, sketching the outline of the dream she hoped to one day live. Reflecting on her romance with Travis, she shared, "This is sort of what I've been writing songs about wanting to happen to me since I was a teenager." A love that once lived only in lyrics has become her reality, reminding us that the wishes we hold closest to our hearts can come true.

TRUE LOVE
SPEAKS YOUR
LANGUAGE.

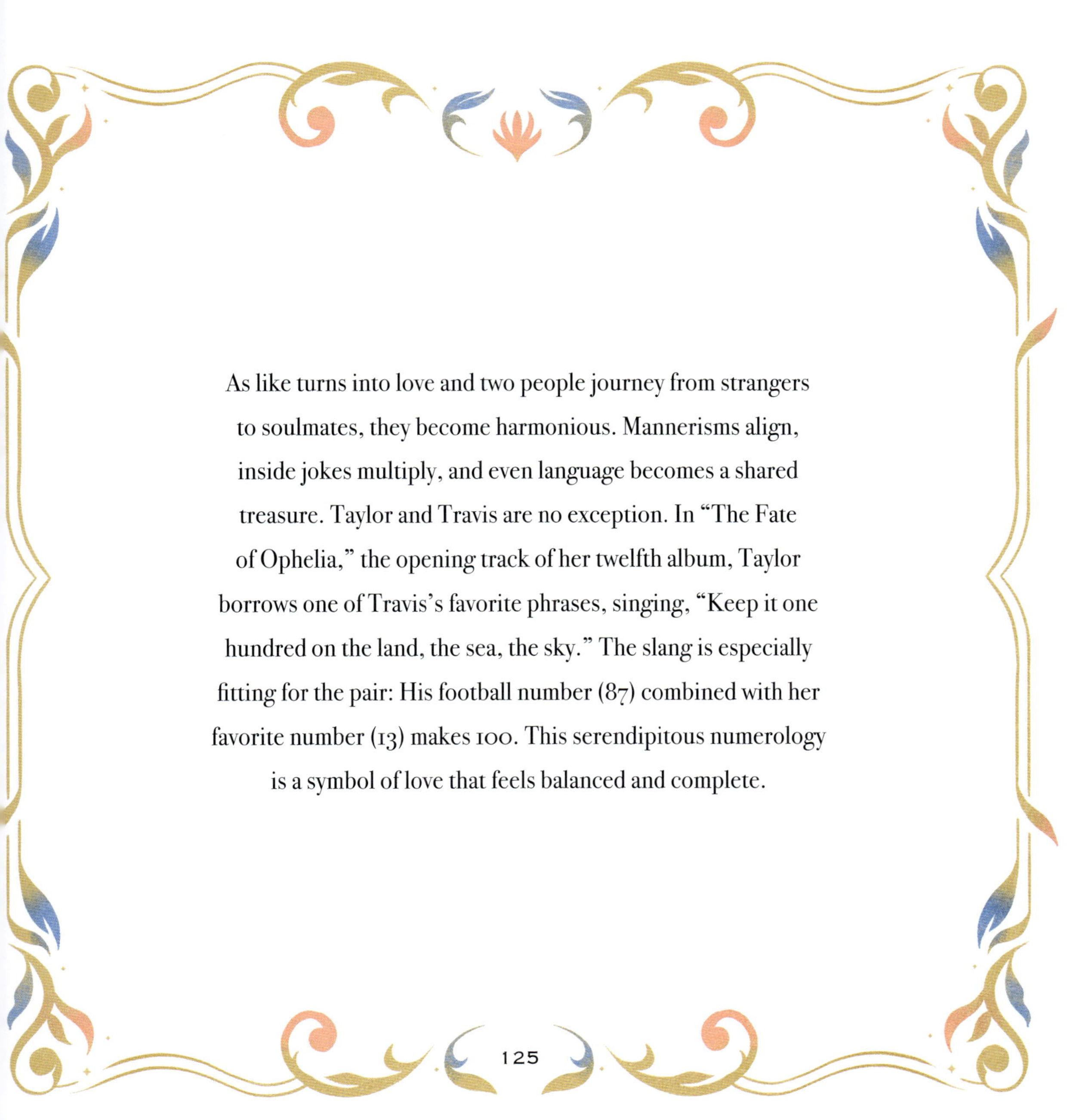

As like turns into love and two people journey from strangers to soulmates, they become harmonious. Mannerisms align, inside jokes multiply, and even language becomes a shared treasure. Taylor and Travis are no exception. In "The Fate of Ophelia," the opening track of her twelfth album, Taylor borrows one of Travis's favorite phrases, singing, "Keep it one hundred on the land, the sea, the sky." The slang is especially fitting for the pair: His football number (87) combined with her favorite number (13) makes 100. This serendipitous numerology is a symbol of love that feels balanced and complete.

TRUE LOVE SAYS FOREVER.

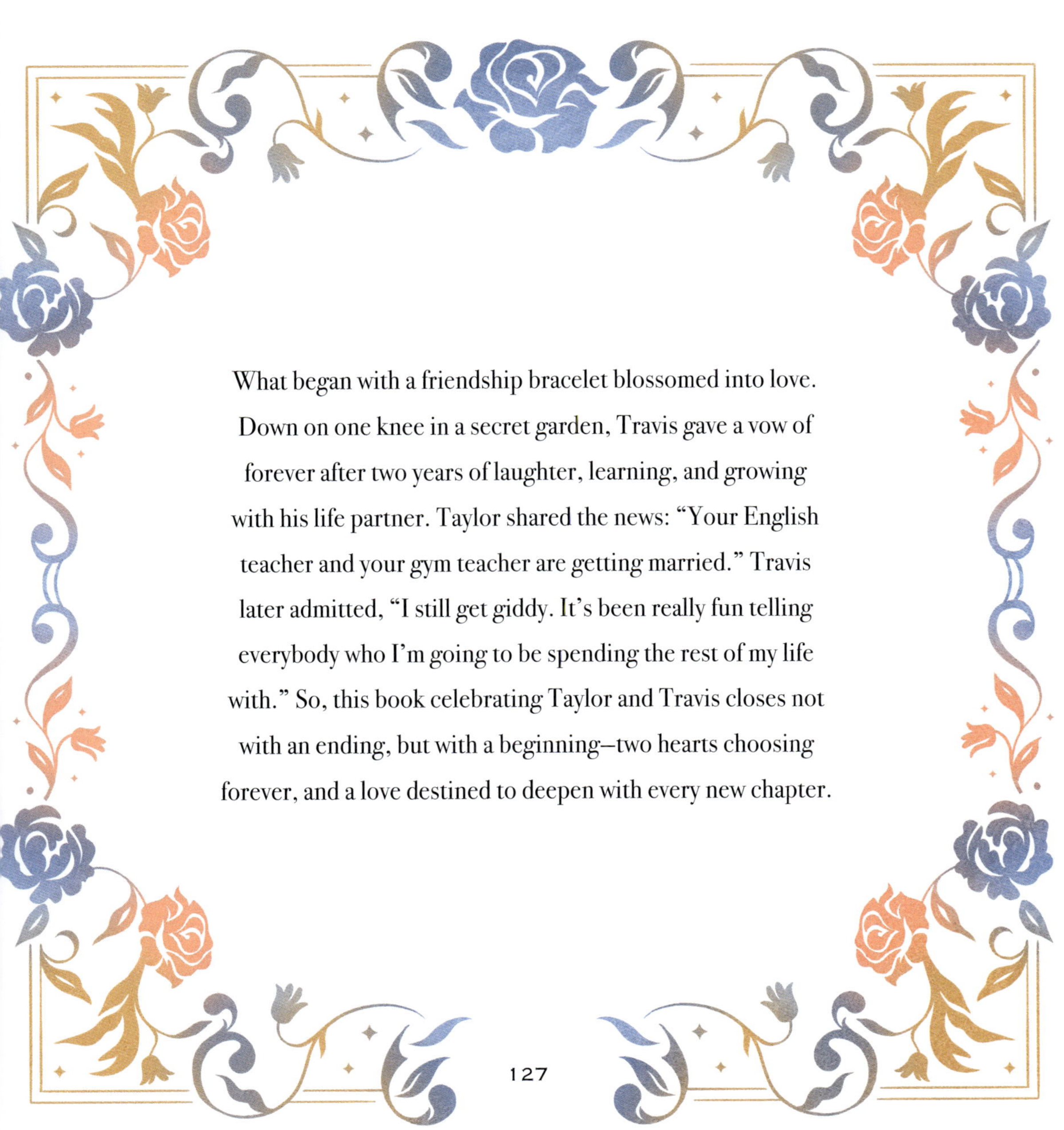

What began with a friendship bracelet blossomed into love. Down on one knee in a secret garden, Travis gave a vow of forever after two years of laughter, learning, and growing with his life partner. Taylor shared the news: "Your English teacher and your gym teacher are getting married." Travis later admitted, "I still get giddy. It's been really fun telling everybody who I'm going to be spending the rest of my life with." So, this book celebrating Taylor and Travis closes not with an ending, but with a beginning–two hearts choosing forever, and a love destined to deepen with every new chapter.

"He's just my favorite person I've ever met—no offense to everyone else. But the fact that this is the person that I get to hang out with every day forever . . . that's the whole thing of it."

—Taylor

"I can't wait to spend the rest of my life with her. She has brought excitement and a joy for life that made me a better man, made me a better person, and made me just that much more comfortable in who I am."

—Travis